Under the Yellow & Red Stars

A MEMOIR

Under the Yellow & Red Stars
Alex Levin

The Azrieli Foundation
164 Eglinton Avenue East, Suite 503
Toronto, Ontario
Canada, M4P 1G4
www.azrielifoundation.org

Cover and book design by Mark Goldstein
Cartography by Karen van Kerkoele

Library and Archives Canada Cataloguing in Publication

Levin, Alex, 1932–
    Under the yellow and red stars/ Alex Levin.

(Azrieli series of Holocaust survivor memoirs. Series II)
Includes bibliographical references and index.
ISBN 978-1-897470-07-7

1. Levin, Alex, 1932–. 2. Holocaust, Jewish (1939–1945) – Poland. 3. Jewish children in the Holocaust – Poland – Biography. 4. Jews – Poland – Biography. 5. Jews – Soviet Union – Biography. I. Azrieli Foundation II. Title. III. Series: Azrieli series of Holocaust survivor memoirs. Series II

D804.196.L49 2009   940.53'18092   C2009-901397-5

© **Mixed Sources**
Product group from well-managed forests, controlled sources and recycled wood or fiber
www.fsc.org Cert no. SW-COC-002080
FSC © 1996 Forest Stewardship Council

Printed in Canada

The Azrieli Series of Holocaust Survivor Memoirs

Contents

Series Preface:
In their own words...

In telling these stories, the writers have liberated themselves. For so many years we did not speak about it, even when we became free people living in a free society. Now, when at last we are writing about what happened to us in this dark period of history, knowing that our stories will be read and live on, it is possible for us to feel truly free. These unique historical documents put a face on what was lost, and allow readers to grasp the enormity of what happened to six million Jews – one story at a time.

David J. Azrieli, C.M., C.Q., MArch
Holocaust survivor and founder, The Azrieli Foundation

Since the end of World War II, over 30,000 Jewish Holocaust survivors have immigrated to Canada. Who they are, where they came from, what they experienced and how they built new lives for themselves and their families are important parts of our Canadian heritage. The Azrieli Foundation-York University Holocaust Survivor Memoirs Program was established to preserve and share the memoirs written by those who survived the twentieth-century Nazi genocide of the Jews of Europe and later made their way to Canada. The program is guided by the conviction that each survivor of the Holocaust has a remarkable story to tell, and that such stories play an important role in education about tolerance and diversity.

Millions of individual stories are lost to us forever. By preserving the stories written by survivors and making them widely available to a broad audience, the Azrieli Series of Holocaust Survivor Memoirs seeks to sustain the memory of all those who perished at the hands of hatred, abetted by indifference and apathy. The personal accounts of those who survived against all odds are as different as the people who wrote them, but all demonstrate the courage, strength, wit and luck that it took to prevail and survive in such terrible adversity. The memoirs are also moving tributes to people – strangers and friends – who risked their lives to help others, and who, through acts of kindness and decency in the darkest of moments, frequently helped the persecuted maintain faith in humanity and courage to endure. These accounts offer inspiration to all, as does the survivors' desire to share their experiences so that new generations can learn from them.

The Holocaust Survivor Memoirs Program collects, archives and publishes these distinctive records and the print editions are available free of charge to libraries, schools and Holocaust-education programs across Canada, and to the general public at Azrieli Foundation educational events. Online editions of the books are available on our web site, www.azrielifoundation.org.

The Israel and Golda Koschitzky Centre for Jewish Studies has provided scholarly assistance and guidance in the preparation of these memoirs for publication. The manuscripts as originally submitted are preserved in the Clara Thomas Archives and Special Collections at York University, and are available for review by interested scholars.

The Azrieli Foundation would like to express deep appreciation to Tamarah Feder, Managing Editor and Program Manager 2005–2008 for her contribution to the establishment of this program and for her work on Series I and II. We also gratefully acknowledge the following people for their invaluable efforts in producing this series: Mary Arvanitakis, Elin Beaumont, François Blanc, Aurélien Bonin, Florence Buathier, Mark Celinscack, Nicolas Côté, Jordana de Bloeme, Darrel Dickson (Maracle Press), Andrea Geddes Poole, Sir Martin Gilbert, Esther Goldberg, Mark Goldstein, Elizabeth Lasserre, Lisa Newman, Carson Phillips, Susan Roitman, Judith Samuels, Randall Schnoor, Erica Simmons, Jody Spiegel, Mia Spiro, Erika Tucker and Karen Van Kerkoerle.

I dedicate this book to my only daughter, Yelena, and my grand-children, Jonathan and Michaela, so that they know about their roots and pass this story on to their children and grandchildren.

I also dedicate this book to the Righteous among the Nations who risked their lives to save Jews; to the Holocaust survivors and their efforts to rebuild their shattered lives; and to my fellow cadets for their friendship through the years.

I would like to thank my wife, Marina, and my brother Samuel for their patience and support during my life journey, and Craig Dershowitz, Howard Cooper, Eugene Grin-Gnotovsky and the staff of Azrieli Foundation for their assistance and advice.

Introduction

Every night, after dark, we crawled cautiously into stacks of hay in the fields, covering ourselves so that the only opening was a small breathing hole. Sometimes we secretly spent the nights in a tool shed. No matter what the circumstances, we were always terrified that we might be caught....

So writes Alex Levin, recollecting the routine terrors of his tenth year of life and drawing us into events and experiences almost unimaginable from the perspective of a safe and sane society years later. From an idyllic childhood in the heart of a "strong and loving family" to a desperate existence fleeing the Nazi genocide, to a military career in the antisemitic post-war Soviet Union, to new roots on Canadian soil, Alex Levin's life bears the tracks of momentous historical shifts. If, as Elie Wiesel reminds us, every Holocaust survivor has a unique story to tell, Alex Levin's story is extraordinary.

Alex Levin – then called Joshua Levin – was born in 1932 in Rokitno, a small town in Poland of five thousand inhabitants. Set in what he describes as "majestic and beautiful surroundings," Levin's early years were bucolic. He lived in a large house with a garden and domestic animals and swam in the river that flowed through the town. He enjoyed exploring the lush oak woods nearby – forests that would soon play a key role in his life and very survival.

In 1939 approximately 3.3 million Jews lived in Poland, by far the largest Jewish population of any country in Europe. Jewish cultural and religious life had flourished there for hundreds of years. Compared to the Jewish experience elsewhere in Europe and Russia, Polish Jews had lived in relative peace with their neighbours. The Jews of Poland were able to develop important religious and national movements, to establish renowned centres of religious learning, and to develop the rich cultural heritage of the Yiddish language – the daily language of Eastern European Jews. By the middle of the twentieth century, the Jews of Poland could boast a distinctive literary tradition that encompassed Yiddish fiction, poetry, theatre and cinema. Moreover, as Poland modernized and urban centres grew, many professions and industries became less restrictive, and opportunities for Jews opened up.

Jewish life in Poland was full of contradictions, however. Polish Jews were often subject to discrimination and persecution, and even physical assault by their non-Jewish neighbours who harboured prejudice against them. With the rise of Polish nationalism between the two world wars, ethnic minorities – Jews among them – found themselves the target of discriminatory practices. Even though the Polish constitution guaranteed the rights of minorities, Jews were barred from holding jobs in government, one of the largest employers at the time. With the impact of the world-wide economic Great Depression that began in the early 1930s, the condition of Polish Jews steadily worsened.

Yet Alex Levin remembers a comfortable and happy upbringing amid Rokitno's 2,000-member-strong Jewish community. As a child, little Shike – a nickname for Yehoshua – was aware of, but not directly touched by, the pernicious anti-Jewish sentiments around him. Like many Jews in the small towns and villages of Poland, Levin's family valued religious education, observed Jewish holidays and other rituals, and savoured the special taste of Sabbath foods. Zionism – the movement to build a Jewish state in the Jews' historic homeland, then under control of the British – was also important to his family. Levin fondly recalls meeting with his youth group, Betar, on the edge of town, singing Hebrew songs and listening to stories of Jewish heroes in their homeland. Founded in 1923 in Latvia, Betar was one of several youth groups that played an important role in the history of Polish Jews in the inter-war period. These groups fought antisemitism and fostered a sense of Jewish identity. Their leaders later played an active part in Jewish resistance in the ghettoes and camps during the war. The youth group gatherings were, in Levin's words, a "magical" time in his life.

In September 1939, everything changed. On September 1, the German army invaded Poland from the west; on September 17, the Soviet army moved in from the east. In late August, Hitler and Stalin had reached an agreement to divide Poland between their two countries. Rokitno, Levin's home town, fell under Soviet rule. As the Red Army moved in, Levin's carefree childhood was over at the tender age of seven.

Life under the Soviets grew difficult for the Jews of Poland. Levin remembers only a few details from this first period of Soviet occupation – for example, the confiscation and nationalization of private enterprises and the prohibition against religious instruction. But Jewish families remained together and in their own homes. In June 1941, however, when Germany invaded the Soviet Union, reneging on the Nazi-Soviet pact and ending the alliance between the two countries, the situation changed drastically. Rokitno was soon occupied by Germany. As the German army moved eastward, special units of the SS and the military police followed behind them, waging an unprecedented campaign of murder against the Jewish civilian population.

The Nazis used the phrase "Final Solution" to describe the murderous anti-Jewish policies they implemented in the territories they occupied. Along with the goal of expanding territorially to the East and subjugating the Slavs, radical and violent antisemitism lay at the heart of Nazi ideology. In this worldview, the Germans were members of a superior "Aryan" race and had the right to rule over others. Jews were defined as the lowest of all peoples and were to be annihilated. Once World War II began, the implementation of the "Final Solution" came in two stages. In the first, which began with the occupation of Poland in 1939 and lasted until June 1941, Jews were deprived of their rights, isolated in ghettoes, forced to wear visible identifying markers, humiliated, starved and exploited. Many died and were killed. In the second phase, which started with the German invasion of the Soviet Union in June 1941, Jews were targeted for total "extermination." Soviet Jews – including those in Levin's home town – were to be methodically slaughtered en masse. Sometimes the killing was preceded by an initial and accelerated stage of ghettoization and forced labour until the resources needed to massacre so many Jews could be assembled. The Nazi policy of systematic mass murder that was first implemented in the USSR was soon extended to other German-occupied and German-allied countries.

Alex Levin recounts the experiences of the Jews of Rokitno from the perspective of the child he was and gives us the everyday details that are not fully apparent from a broad-strokes history of Nazi policies. Levin recollects with poignant clarity the establishment of the Rokitno ghetto, the requirement that Jews wear yellow Star of David badges, the confiscation of possessions, the forced labour, the starvation. Like other children, Alex put his life at risk to sneak out of the ghetto and barter what few possessions his family retained for food to keep them alive. Levin describes in chilling detail the day Rokitno's Jews were murdered. On August 26, 1942, after living under a reign of terror for just over a year, the Jews of Rokitno were ordered to gather in the central square for deportation to a killing site outside the town. When many of them realized what was about to occur, the crowd began to panic. As people began to run, Nazi and Ukrainian police began to shoot. In the chaos that ensued, young Alex and his older brother Samuel ran – as fast and as "far away from that murderous place as possible."

Apart from the few Rokitno Jews who, like the two Levin brothers, managed to flee into the woods, those who were not massacred that day in the town square were deported to Sarny, some forty kilometres away. There, over the course of four days in late August 1942, Nazi killing squads claimed the lives of over 18,000 Jews. By this time the implementation of the "Final Solution" was well on its way. Historians estimate that approximately 2.7 million Jews lived in the Soviet territories occupied by the Germans in 1941. When these areas were liberated in 1943 and 1944, only 100,000 to 120,000 Jews had survived. Most were killed in mass shooting operations, though many also perished in the death camps established by the Nazis further to the west.

Against this backdrop, the escape of the two Levin boys is nothing short of miraculous. Their parents dead, their friends and relatives killed or taken away to parts unknown, the two boys desperately fled ruthless Nazi troops and eluded local collaborators, chief among them Ukrainians. Many Ukrainian nationalists, particularly in western Ukraine, saw the German invasion of the Soviet Union as a means to liberate the Ukraine from Soviet and Polish control. Fuelled by nationalist hopes as well as a long history of antisemitism, they abetted the Nazi genocide.

Other Jews also escaped the Nazi genocide by fleeing into the forests. By 1944 the densely wooded areas of eastern Poland and the Ukraine emerged as the Jews' only haven, their last chance for survival. Against all odds, these fugitives in the forests remained alive for years, avoiding the Nazis, marauding bandits and brutal Nazi collaborators. Isolated and hunted, they struggled to find food and endured harsh and primitive conditions. Scholars estimate that some 100,000 Jews escaped into the forests of Poland, Russia, the Ukraine, Lithuania and Belorussia, and that 25,000 of them survived. Many of them joined partisan groups – irregular, independent fighting units that resisted the Nazis and their allies, disrupting German communication lines and bravely conducting sabotage operations. By 1944, there were probably 250,000 partisan fighters operating hundreds of brigades in eastern Poland, western Russia and the Ukraine.

Levin was only ten years old when he and his seventeen-year-old brother Samuel escaped into the woods. Unable to find a partisan unit that would take them, the two boys hid out for eighteen months. Soon meeting up with a few other Jews who had also escaped the Rokitno massacre, the fugitives devised an ingeniously camouflaged hole in the ground, deep in the dense woods, and managed to find food, make clothing and survive – they even managed to establish some sense of routine. As Levin notes, under other circumstances it would have been an adventure; as it was, they withstood unimaginable terror and hardship. Most of the Jews who escaped into the forests were killed by Nazi patrols, local inhabitants or antisemitic partisans. Others died of starvation, illness, or froze to death in the harsh winter. "Death," Levin writes, "was a real part of our lives in the forest." Yet despite its terrors, the young boy began to make friends with the forest, whose dark depths sheltered him from those who wished to murder him. Robbed of his family, his home, his community, and denied the protection that society should offer its citizens, young Shike found that the woods became his "fortress," his "best friend," his "refuge and hearth." Levin's resilience and his identification with his surroundings are compelling. "The woods gave us life," he writes. "They saved us." His story is a testament to his will to survive.

Levin's account of his survival is particularly valuable because it offers a rare and special perspective on the Holocaust. Few Jewish children survived the Nazi murder machine; even fewer survived hiding in the woods for an extended period of time. The occasional kindness of a peasant or partisan allowed the boys to live another day; more often the cruelty of the local population added to their torment. We learn from Levin, as we have from other survivor testimony, the perilousness of Jewish life in Nazi-occupied lands. Many Poles and Ukrainians behaved no less sadistically than the Germans. Those who attempted to shelter Jews or provide them with food put their own lives at risk, as was the case with two Poles – Ludwik Wrodarczyk and Felicia Masojada – who were murdered by collaborators for helping the Levin boys and others. Ultimately it was the Red Army that rescued Alex. In January of 1944, after a year and a half in hiding, Levin emerged from the woods with the Soviet troops who found him. Taking pity on the eleven-year-old orphan who had nowhere to go, Soviet officials invited him to join the 13th Army as a helper in a field hospital unit. Because his Yiddish nickname, Shike, was unfamiliar to Russian ears, he was dubbed Shura or Shurik, both diminutive forms of Alexander. Soon Alexander became his formal new name. For the next year Levin was a "son of the regiment," accompanying Soviet troops across Poland and into Germany, tending the sick and wounded. Travelling with the Red Army he came to fully understand the fate of his family and the murdered Jews of Poland, and also the price of war. His descriptions of these experiences offer a rare window into the behaviour of Soviet soldiers in this period, both good and bad. The same troops who adopted and cared for Alex also looted and raped the civilian population of their now-defeated enemy. Still, it is the affection and warmth of the people in his unit that is most apparent. These "courageous, sensitive and honest people" gave him a renewed feeling of community. The army became his family, his first home after the forest.

In April 1945, the war ended for Alex. He was ordered to Moscow with other young war orphans now under the care of the Red Army and given the opportunity to go to school and pick up the broken strands of his life. If Levin's memoir had ended with his journey to Moscow, it would be an important contribution to our understanding of both the suffering of Jewish children during these years and the harsh nature of survival in the forests of Eastern Europe, far from civilization. But Levin's journey does not cease in 1945 with the defeat of Nazi Germany. Rather, he explores his post-war life in the Soviet Union and offers us a further glimpse not only of an extraordinary man with an unusual path, but of the turns of history.

As the war ended, Levin dreamed of a military career. Inspired by the care and courage of those who took him in during the final year and a half of the war, he viewed military service as a means to avenge and honour the memory of his family and save future innocent people from victimization. He also felt a strong sense of gratitude to the Soviet Union. In this he was not alone: the Soviet Union became a sanctuary of sorts for Jews fleeing the Nazis during the Holocaust. An estimated one million Jews eluded the genocidal net in this way, among them Levin's older brother Natan. Although many of these refugees were viewed with suspicion and sent to labour camps in Siberia, this forced displacement also saved their lives. Other Jewish refugees survived in the USSR and, like Levin, joined in the fight against the Nazis. Following his dream, Levin entered the prestigious Suvorov Military School in the fall of 1945 at the age of thirteen. There, he forged long-lasting friendships, achieved academic success and, after two more years in infantry training school, emerged as an officer in the vaunted Red Army. But Levin's life in the Soviet Union did not live up to the promise of acceptance he had felt as a son of the regiment and as a star student at the military school. Instead, he came of age at the height of a renewed campaign of antisemitic persecution, this time directed by Joseph Stalin. In an ironic twist of history, the Soviet Union won a decisive victory over its greatest enemy – the Nazis – only to incorporate the core of that enemy's political program – antisemitism – into its own policies. Having survived the yellow stars of the Nazis, Alex Levin found himself confronting the red stars of the Soviet Union.

The years immediately following World War II were characterized by social and political repression in the Soviet Union that had severe implications for its Jewish population. Antisemitism, of course, was not a new phenomenon in Russia. Jews under tsarist rule in the Russian Empire contended with religious persecution and restrictions in education, profession and residence. At the end of the nineteenth century, these persecutions turned deadly as two waves of government sanctioned pogroms – in 1881 and again in 1903 – made Jewish life in tsarist Russia untenable. Because of the oppression they experienced, many Jews became active in the Russian Revolution, which promised a society based on egalitarian principles. And, indeed, with the overthrow of tsarist rule, Vladimir Lenin condemned antisemitism. Although the new regime was hostile to religion generally, the social, economic and political situation for Jews improved.

By the late 1920s, however, the rise of Joseph Stalin brought about a new period of repression. Seeking to consolidate his power and transform the USSR into a modern industrialized state, Stalin introduced a "revolution from above" and an era of political terror. Virtually every family in the USSR experienced the consequences of Stalin's brutal policies, which included collectivization, forced industrialization, mass population transfers, political purges, mass arrests and executions. By the end of the 1930s, Stalin's policies had claimed 20 million victims. Under Stalin, the Soviet Union emerged as one of the world's great police states. Fear became an essential part of everyday life. In this terrorized society, Jews were frequently singled out. Indeed, while lip-service was paid to the cultural "autonomy" of the different nationalities in the USSR – with "Jew" (in Russian, *Yevrei*) included as a nationality – in reality any ethnic or national group with characteristics or aspirations that showed them to be separate or different from the greater collective met with suspicion and persecution. This rather large set included Crimean Tatars, "kulaks" (prosperous, land-owning peasants) and many others as well as Jews. While historians do not doubt Stalin's personal antipathy toward Jews, his persecution – in contrast to Hitler's – was not racially dogmatic.

The Soviet Union's life-and-death struggle with Nazi Germany changed the atmosphere of political, social and cultural repression in the USSR. The army relied upon the loyalty and support of a wide range of its constituent ethnic and national groups, and minorities – including Jews – quickly experienced a relaxation of the pre-war pressures and restrictions. As long as the USSR was pitted against

Nazi Germany, Stalin appealed to the patriotism of the Soviet citizenry, playing down communist ideology to win support for the Great Patriotic War, as Russians call their conflict with Germany in World War ii. Many groups that earlier had been persecuted, disenfranchised, deported and murdered now found themselves rehabilitated. Drafted into the army, they courageously fought for their country. It is estimated that over half a million Jews fought in the Red Army and perhaps 100,000 were killed in action. Alex Levin met many of these Jewish servicemen and women when he travelled with the Red Army. In this atmosphere, it is notable that Alex rarely encountered ideological or antisemitic rhetoric as a son of the regiment or even as a young cadet in the military school.

Many ordinary Soviet citizens hoped that more tolerant policies would ensue after the war ended. Soon after the German defeat, however, Stalin initiated an era of renewed ideological vigilance that had harsh consequences for Jews. In 1948, a new campaign against "alien influences" took aim at several groups that included the intelligentsia, artists, writers and musicians. Anyone who might influence opinion on cultural matters now had to conform to a strict party line. As part of this policy, Jews too were directly and openly targeted in a deadly campaign of slanderous accusations, arrests, executions and deportations. The state-controlled media called for the elimination of "cosmopolitanism" and "bourgeois individualism" that threatened Soviet collective ideals; it also singled out "rootless cosmopolitans" – an encoded reference to Jews. With the flames of ideological and antisemitic fervour actively fanned, the next five years saw a deadly increase in official antisemitic acts by the government, along with violence on the part of ordinary citizens against their Jewish neighbours.

The decision of the Soviet leadership to crack down once again rather than to liberalize says much about the deep insecurity of the USSR in the immediate post-war period. Although the country emerged victorious, it had lost an estimated 30 million people in the war and its industrial and transport infrastructure was destroyed.

The Soviet Union now faced years of economic hardship. These challenges were exacerbated by a severe drought in 1946 and an ensuing famine that caused another estimated 1.5 million deaths. In addition, many Soviet citizens had encountered the more prosperous and open Western European culture for the first time while serving in the Red Army. Stalin feared that this exposure might lead to agitation for change. These pressures led Soviet authorities to cordon off the USSR from outside influences.

Levin's memoir offers personal insight into this highly charged period. As a young cadet at the military school soon after the war, he was more concerned with classes, drills, sports and girls than with politics and ideology. But he had a growing awareness of the deteriorating atmosphere, particularly when he learned that one of his important mentors had been targeted in the new campaign and killed by the Soviet secret police. Renowned Jewish actor and director Solomon Mikhoels was the head of the Jewish Anti-Fascist Committee (JAFC), a group of well-known Jewish cultural figures established at Stalin's behest to influence international public opinion and organize political and material support for the Soviet war effort in the West, especially in the United States and Canada. Toward the end of the war, the JAFC began to document and speak publicly about the mass murder of Jews in the Nazi genocide. Official Soviet policy did not acknowledge the genocide of the Jews, however; instead, the official view was that atrocities were committed against all Soviet citizens. Both the JAFC's wartime contact with Americans to aid the Soviet war effort and their insistence on acknowledging the Jewish victims of Nazism, made them a prime target for persecution in the post-war crackdown. Soon after Mikhoel's murder, the other members of the JAFC were also arrested, imprisoned and executed. By 1952–1953, the campaign had reached a fevered pitch. In 1952, for example, thirteen prominent Yiddish writers were executed on false charges of treason and espionage in an event known as the "Night of the Murdered Poets." The following year Stalin targeted Jewish doctors in the so-called Doctors Plot as a prelude to yet another major deadly purge. Scholars believe that a massive deportation of Jews to eastern Siberia would have ensued had Stalin not died in March 1953.

These worsening conditions indicated the depth of official Soviet suspicion of Jews, a suspicion that was strengthened by the development of a sense of solidarity among Soviet Jews with the Jewish victims of the Holocaust and their growing identity as Jews. It was also exacerbated by the establishment of the State of Israel in 1948, which gave Soviet Jews a foreign homeland. Although the Soviet Union had initially supported the creation of the State of Israel, Soviet opposition to the United States in the Cold War complicated foreign relations with the new country. The assumption that Soviet Jews had conflicting loyalties combined with Soviet support for Egypt and Syria meant that superpower conflict over the Middle East often affected the USSR's internal policies toward the Jewish community.

Stalin's anti-Jewish campaign formed the backdrop for Alex Levin's graduation from the Suvorov Military School and his early career in the military. Indeed, although young Alex was aware of what was going on while he was at the military academy, he was still taken by surprise when, in 1951, Stalin's antisemitic policies touched him personally. In the spring of that year, the nineteen-year-old Levin graduated close to the top of his class but was denied the prestigious commission he had earned. Instead, he was placed on a second-rate career track, with all choice appointments and promotions remaining just outside of his grasp. No matter how hard he worked or how well he performed, his opportunities would remain limited, solely because he was Jewish. The sense that his adopted and genuinely beloved homeland had betrayed him would never leave him.

Levin's constant and demoralizing confrontation with officially sanctioned antisemitism in the 1950s and 1960s demonstrates that even after other elements of Stalinism had been dismantled, prejudice against Jews remained active government policy in the USSR. Levin and other Soviet Jews, simply by virtue of being Jews, were regarded as security risks and potentially traitorous. On that presumption, they were excluded from political life and from certain careers and professions, including the army, the secret police, and the party apparatus. Precisely at a time when their talents were desperately needed, patriotic and committed young people such as Alex Levin were banned from contributing to Soviet society. The professional and political discrimination against Jews added to the long-standing restrictions on religious education and Jewish cultural and religious life. The Soviet government continued to actively use the media and other vehicles of propaganda to stigmatize Jews. Although the consequences were less deadly than they had been under Stalin, the Soviet Union was a country, as Levin notes, in which "there was no present and no future" for Jewish survivors of the Holocaust.

Levin's situation became intolerable when Israel defeated Egypt and Syria, both Soviet client states, in the 1967 Six-Day War. He had long known that his two surviving brothers lived in Israel, and his longing to know more about them and make contact conflicted with the fact that these "foreign connections" could place him under a cloud of suspicion. When his brother Samuel's wife came to Moscow to visit him in 1964, he was monitored by the feared Soviet counter-intelligence services. After the 1967 war, the existence of these relatives brought his military career to a full stop.

Within a few years, like many other Soviet Jews who bore the brunt of government oppression, Levin sought the right to emigrate. By the 1970s, thousands of Jews had begun applying for exit visas to leave the Soviet Union. The very act of applying was risky: once they applied, they were considered traitors to the Soviet Union. They were frequently fired from their jobs, as were most of their family members, and they were often forced out of their homes. Without employment, they were categorized as "social parasites," a criminal offence in the Soviet Union. The vast majority of applicants were refused permission to emigrate, moreover, and became known as "refuseniks." Soviet treatment of the refuseniks sparked mass protest demonstrations in many Western countries. Eventually the Kremlin relented, granting some of the refuseniks exit visas. Levin was among the lucky ones who were never refused. He left the Soviet Union in 1974 with a welter of clashing emotions. So many significant memories were bound up in the country that had first offered him safe haven. But he was eager to trade the persecution and oppression of the Soviet Union for freedom and equality in Canada. In 1975, he arrived in Toronto.

Levin's complicated feelings mirror those of many Jewish refugees from the Soviet Union. Saved by the Red Army or by escaping into the Soviet Union, many Jews from pre-war Poland felt appreciation and even love for their country of refuge. Levin conveys his profound gratitude towards the Red Army and those who offered him support and community, including the military academy that became a surrogate family and home. His memoir makes clear how much he wanted to serve the USSR after the war. But if the Soviets saved Alex Levin's life, they never truly liberated him. The official antisemitic restrictions that came into force around the time he graduated from the military academy demonstrated that his new country did not fully accept him. His experiences during the Cold War reinforced this. Levin's true liberation came only when he reached Canada.

Like many immigrants to Canada, Alex Levin found that the path to full integration into Canadian society offered a mixture of challenges and opportunities. He needed to adapt to an entirely new system that was so unlike the one he had mastered in the Soviet Union. In addition to negotiating life in a new language, he had to learn to navigate different sets of professional norms, different ways of managing finances and a different legal system. Like many other new Canadians, he committed himself to building a new Canadian life, working hard to lay down new roots for his family. As a Canadian, he was free – in ways he had not been in the Soviet Union – to identify with the Canadian Jewish community, with whom he shared a sense of history and a hope for the future.

Levin's memoir reminds us of the preciousness of recollections such as his – stories of those who came away from a tragic universe of death and destruction, with losses that cannot be made whole. The tale of an ordinary boy and man who cut a heroic figure while facing extraordinary circumstances, Levin's is also the larger story of Jewish resistance and survival against great odds through his personal remembrance.

Alex Levin's life reflects a series of homes established and then dismantled, of roots laid down only to be continually uprooted. The warmth of his childhood home in Rokitno, the love of his family, the friendships of his youth group are all shattered by external forces, lost to him forever. His precarious home in the deep forest, terrifying but also sustaining, gives way to the protection of the Soviet army as it moves westward into a defeated Germany. The camaraderie of the Red Army and the care shown this young war orphan reestablishes the bonds of human connection for Alex. That, too, comes to a close with the end of World War II. The sense of cohesion and purpose in the Soviet military, with its mix of discrimination and prejudice but also appreciation and advancement, comes apart for Alex because of the inner contradictions between the promise of egalitarianism and the lack of tolerance for Jewishness. The home he establishes with his wife breaks apart not once but twice under pressure from an oppressive and controlling regime that turns on its citizens. Finally, on Canadian soil, Levin rebuilds his home, his family, and his life one final time as his wife and daughter join him in a leap of faith into their Canadian future.

Alex Levin attributes his survival against such overwhelming odds to luck. Certainly, luck was a significant factor, as it was in the lives of all survivors of the Holocaust. But Levin also survived because of his own extraordinary resilience and resourcefulness, and because of the kindness and courage of others at crucial moments. One could say that Levin's life presented him with the extremes in human nature

– the very worst behaviour and the very best; murderous cruelty and life-saving kindness. He observes that "The evil is easier to remember than the good." But his memoir recollects as well the courageous people he encountered, the "true good souls" who put their lives on the line to save him and others from genocide. To read Alex Levin's memoir is to follow his tracks in a world where ethical choices matter deeply. It is a call to remember the past and to instill hope for the future.

Naomi Azrieli
Sara R. Horowitz
2009

The authors would like to thank Irving Abella for his contribution to an earlier version of this introduction.

SOURCES:

Arad, Yitzhak. "The Destruction of the Jews in German-Occupied Territories in the Soviet Union," in *The Unknown Black Book: The Holocaust in the German-Occupied Soviet Territories,* eds. Joshua Rubenstein and Ilya Altman. Bloomington: Indiana University Press, 2008.

Conquest, Robert. *The Great Terror: A Reassessment.* New York: Oxford University Press, 1990.

Friedlander, Saul. *The Years of Extermination: Nazi Germany and the Jews, 1939–1945.* New York: Harper Collins, 2007.

Gittleman Zvi. *A Century of Ambivalence: The Jews of Russia and the Soviet Union, 1881 to the Present.* Bloomington: Indiana University Press, 2001.

Laqueur, Walter, ed. *The Holocaust Encyclopedia.* New Haven: Yale University Press, 2001.

Pinkus, Benjamin. *The Jews of the Soviet Union.* Cambridge University Press, 2003.

Redlich, Shimon, ed. *War, Holocaust and Stalinism: A Documented History of the Jewish Anti-Fascist Committee in the USSR.* Oxford: Taylor and Francis, 1995.

Ro'i Ya'akov, ed. *Jews and Jewish Life in Russia and the Soviet Union.* Oxford: Taylor and Francis, 1995.

Rozett, Robert and Shmuel Spector, eds. *Encyclopedia of the Holocaust*. Jerusalem: Yad Vashem and The Jerusalem Publishing House, 2000.

Service, Robert. *A History of Twentieth-Century Russia*. Cambridge: Harvard University Press, 1999.

I want you to write this book. Since you've decided to be faithful to your life, to the memory of it, don't deviate from your chosen path.

YURI NAGIBIN

Author's Preface

My senses have not left me.

I can still see the war-ravaged faces of hate all around me. I can see the blood. I can smell the sickening pall of gun smoke rising towards the sky after having cracked the air with its evil. Blunt sticks are raised to the sky, held high in bloodied hands, before crashing down again. I hear the dogs baying with bared fangs, leaping towards the same indifferent sky, straining to break free of their chains and join in the carnage all around them. I hear the subdued murmur of confusion and fear followed by desperate shrieks of pain. Worse, I hear the final cries of death from innocent victims. I know these victims to be my friends: children who had months earlier played with me after school, neighbours who had borrowed things and lent them, teachers and rabbis who had taught us love and honour.

I feel my brother's hand, trembling but strong, grab onto mine. I hear his words, urging me to run, take hold of my body and move my legs. We run, his hand holding mine with the strength of all the love and honour that had somehow managed to survive. I still imagine that it grasps mine as I write these words now. It has the strength of a thousand men, maybe six million men, but to me it feels like freedom. For the briefest second, we are victorious and I can savour the sweetness of escape. Then, nestled safely in the womb of scrub in the forest, I think of my mother and taste the nauseating acid of anger and irrevocable loss.

My senses have not left me.

~

To write a book that captures the grand scale of events of the past is a thankless if not impossible task. I find it hard not to sink into the details, not to give way to emotions and succumb to illusions. I got the urge to put my story on paper a long time ago and I have been jotting down separate episodes every now and then, albeit with difficulty. But the main motivation for this book came from Elie Wiesel, who said that every person who suffered under the Nazi regime has a unique story and urged us to write it all down.

I have reached the conclusion that such books are extremely useful. Not only do they leave a truthful account of the past for future generations, they also help the people who read them to evaluate life in the present. I know that this will be a testament from those of us who lived to those who were murdered.

In this book I tell the story of an ordinary Jewish family caught up in the events of World War II and the Holocaust. It is the story of three brothers who survived but were separated for more than thirty years. It is the story of our survival despite the cruel and mighty forces that were aimed against us. How we escaped the executions. How we wandered, homeless, from one village to the next, from one settlement to the other. How we found food in a wilderness environment. What our relationships were with the local people.

How is it possible that in the twentieth century two children could live, primitively and in isolation, in the forest for nearly a year and a half, persecuted by a merciless enemy who wanted to kill us, and still survive? And, after all that, how was I able to survive Stalin's dictatorial regime?

More than half a century has passed. Human nature is such that with age our memory begins to fail. The world of the past is fading rapidly and will soon be buried in the annals of history. I have to find strength within me to live through the pain once again. The pain, which is hard to talk about, is even harder to write about. This pain has penetrated my flesh and blood. It is something I've always felt and still experience daily. My memories are hard to fit into easy phrases.

I remember reading that memory is like a ball of yarn. Tug at the thread and it begins to unwind. But the threads of memory tear, bundle up, intertwine. It takes time to get it all in order. I remember only certain details, facts that pulsate in my memory. All my life I tried to forget the past. Anger would boil inside me whenever painful questions about my past arose. I always felt the futility of trying to explain to anyone what happened because they hadn't experienced those horrors firsthand and were unlikely to comprehend the depth of my emotions. One might ask why I still believe in human kindness after all that I've been through.

Holocaust survivors revitalize history simply by being alive. But for a long time the Holocaust itself was not fully reflected in history because the survivors were silent. We weren't ready to talk about our experiences. We were too close to the actual events, our wounds were still fresh. All our energy was aimed toward the future. But perhaps the most important reason for our silence was that no one was ready to really listen to us.

The years went by fast. Now, looking back, when I try to analyze what my childhood and adolescence was actually like, I always say that it was both happy and unhappy at the same time. Nazism and the Soviet dictatorship caused unhappiness. Happiness came from the kind people I met and from my friends.

My generation is the last to have known personally those who risked their lives to fight against the horrors of the Holocaust. It is our solemn responsibility to pass this knowledge on to our children and grandchildren. The period of silence is over. The world has to know exactly what happened during those dark times in order prevent it from ever happening again. We have to bring up the younger generations in freedom to save them from having to go through what our generation went through. We have to teach the youth of today the value of unity and brotherhood. We have to convince them that by treating others well – unconditionally – our lives are enriched and each one of us becomes a more beautiful person. As Martin Bormann, son of Hitler's ruthless second-in-command, has said, "Only if we remember our past will we be able to live in the present and hope to build a new tomorrow." We must live with all the energy and conviction of a promising future.

In the Shtetl of Rokitno

Only be careful, and watch yourselves closely so that you do not forget the things your eyes have seen or let them slip from your heart as long as you live. Teach them to your children and to their children after them.

DEUTERONOMY 4:9

I was born in the small Polish town of Rokitno[1] in 1932 and when World War II began, I was only seven years old. The part of the town where my family lived was predominantly Jewish. I lived there with my father, Mordechai, and my mother, Mindl, and my three brothers – Natan, who was ten years older than me, Samuel, who was seven years older, and Moishe, who was five years younger.

Although Rokitno was a poor and simple place, it was set in majestic and beautiful surroundings. There was a tiny river that was a popular spot with young people. There were wells with unforgettable pure, cold water. There was a park and even an old castle encircled by huge oaks. All around the village, serving as both a barrier and a resource was a lush, thick, overgrown old forest that was by far the most important feature of the locale.

---

1 The town of Rokitno where Alex Levin spent his very early life was about twenty kilometres from the Polish-Soviet border of 1939, and is now part of Ukraine.

Jewish history in Poland dates back a thousand years and the history of Rokitno was bigger in scale than its size might have suggested. Initially a small village, a new town was established on the edge of the old village when a glass factory and railway were built at the turn of the twentieth century. It was Jewish businessmen who brought prosperity to our little town. Eliahu Michaelovitch Rosenberg from Belgium built the Rokitno glass factory around 1899 and the plant became the monopoly supplier of bottles for the state vodka factories. The local sand, rich in silicone, made our town an attractive site for the glass factory and it provided jobs for many local people – Jews, Poles and Ukrainians. Rokitno was also chosen for economic reasons – the massive forest surrounding the location provided cheap wood for fuel, and the fact that this area was considered to be the middle of nowhere at that time allowed for cheap labour. A railway line to the town was completed in 1902.

The first settlers who migrated to the new town of Rokitno were primarily Jews and among these first settlers was my grandfather Sheptl Levin, who, like his father, was a rabbi and shochet – that is, someone trained to slaughter animals so that the meat is kosher.[2] In 1913, the community elected my grandfather to go to Palestine – or Eretz Israel as we called it – to buy land on behalf of Jews in Rokitno who planned to move there. These settlers were mostly dependent on local farmers who sold them surplus grain and local blacksmiths who shoed their horses, and on local trades people and merchants for the exchange of other important services. But despite the mutual benefits, the relationship between Jews and other local people was tense.

The woods surrounding Rokitno played a major role in the life of the Jewish community. Famous for thousand-year-old oak trees,

---

2 Observant Jews follow a system of rules about what to eat, how to prepare food and how meat and poultry are slaughtered (known as Kashruth or "keeping kosher").

the forests were a source of raw material for the local woodcutting shop that was owned by Jews. This area, with its generous harvests of white mushrooms and various berries, was a jewel of Polesie.[3] Jewish entrepreneurs dried, sorted and sold the mushrooms to travelling salesmen.

Our house was just like the majority of the houses in the town. It was fairly large, with a vegetable garden and a separate tool shed. Most Jewish families had domestic animals such as cows, chickens, geese and ducks. They also grew their own vegetables. If we needed anything else we bought it at the market. Our town was known for a volunteer fire brigade with both Polish and Jewish volunteers. Fires were a great danger to our town because most houses were made of wood with straw roofs. The town was also famous for the pharmacy run by the Soltzman family, and people used to come from distant villages to buy medicine prescribed by our doctor, Anischuk.

The population of our town in 1939 was about 8,500. The majority were Poles, with the next largest group being Catholic and Orthodox Christian Ukrainians. Jews made up the third largest group and numbered about 2,000, followed by Russians, Belorussians, Czechs and Gypsies (now known as Roma), although the latter only passed through the town. Jewish community life before the war revolved around two synagogues. The younger children attended an Orthodox primary school, or cheder, and the older children attended a Jewish Tarbut[4] school that taught most subjects in Hebrew. Hebrew was the

---

3 Also known as Polesia, Polesie is the largest swampy lowland area in Europe. It lies mainly within present-day Belarus and Ukraine but also reaches into parts of Poland and Russia. It is a vast expanse of saturated sandy lowlands, low-lying bogs and marshes, and dense forests intersected by a network of rivers.

4 Tarbut was a Zionist network of secular Hebrew-language schools – kindergartens, elementary schools, secondary schools and adult education programs – that operated primarily in Poland, Romania and Lithuania between World War I and World War II. The Tarbut school in Rokitno was founded in the 1920s. For more information, see the glossary.

language of instruction, but Polish language and literature were mandatory subjects. I still remember learning a Polish poem by Adam Mickiewicz: "Zimno, zimno, mróz na dworze, jak do pieca, drzew nołozym, będzie ciepio i milutko, będzie, będzie, ale krótko." (Cold, cold frost on the road, when wood goes into the oven, it will be warm and nice, but only for a short time.)

Polish Jewish life before World War II was rich with religious, cultural and political organizations, including Zionist organizations. As they did throughout Poland, the Jewish community of Rokitno tried to teach their young people to love Jewish culture. Youngsters learned Yiddish and ancient Jewish languages such as Hebrew and Aramaic. There were also a number of people who, after the founding of the World Zionist Organization in 1897, prepared to move to Palestine for good. When my brothers and I were small we were members of the Zionist youth organization Betar.[5] We used to get together with older Betar members and go into the woods surrounding the town and sing Hebrew songs. Sometimes we were joined by Betar members called *halutzim* (pioneers) who actually came from Palestine. I remember singing, "Anu olim Arza, be-shir-u-be-zimra." (We are going to the land of Israel with songs and music.)

These words and the dream of a life in Palestine made a deep and lifelong impression on us. The songs of Betar, the joy of friendship and the promise of uniting together in a homeland made this a magical time for us, perhaps because I was so young and the poignant fantasy of a far away, almost mystical land was enthralling. Perhaps it was because the words of the Hebrew songs were sometimes exotic and mysterious. But, most of all, I remember the feeling of being with a group of friends who shared something in common: a goal and a future.

---

5   Betar is the youth movement created by Revisionist Zionists in 1923. The Betar branch that Alex Levin and his two older brother belonged to was founded in Rokitno in 1928. For more on Betar and Revisionist Zionism, see the glossary.

Our house was at 11 Piłsudski Street in the older part of town that was mostly Jewish. The street was named after Poland's first and most revered leader after the country achieved independence in 1918, but when the Red Army arrived in September 1939, they renamed it Stalin Street.[6] Rokitno didn't have a sewage system, so rainwater always flooded the streets and the town was full of mud all year round. For us boys the floods were an invitation to play and navigate little handmade boats in the puddles. Perhaps if I had lived in the village as an adult I wouldn't have liked the mud so much, but a healthy child only thinks of play.

The mud wasn't the only source of happiness in Rokitno. On Sundays we enjoyed a colourful weekly market in the square in the centre of the new part of town. Hundreds of peasants would come to the market dressed in their best clothes and carrying their goods in willow baskets. Some walked and others filled the streets with their horse carts. Trading happened all around the market square as well as in little Jewish-owned shops. There was so much noise and activity that the market square looked like a boiling sea.

We had a special guest room in our house that we rented to commercial travellers passing through town. My mother also cooked for them, which supplemented our family income. I remember my mother sending Natan out to the train station to look for travelling salesmen to board with us for the night. Our house also had a wholesale textile shop attached to it that was owned by the Haichkes family who rented half of our house from us. The Haichkes used to pay me to hang around the shop and watch the visitors to make sure they didn't steal anything. I remember waiting with such anticipation for Sunday to arrive as I was eager to spend the little money I made on candy or ice cream at the market.

---

6 Marshal Józef Piłsudski led the independent Second Polish Republic from 1918 to 1935. Joseph Stalin was the leader of the Soviet Union from the late 1920s until his death in 1953. For more information, see the glossary.

Our family was a strong and happy one. My mother was the very image of a Jewish mother with her everyday, homey routines. My father, an entrepreneur who travelled throughout our region selling dried edible mushrooms and medicinal herbs, was always concerned for our well-being and our future. My older brothers studied and worked a little here and there.

My oldest brother, Natan, was a jovial boy who loved to play physical games and often came home very dirty. But his main passion was for the pet doves that he kept in a special cage next to the tool shed. Natan had to climb up onto the roof of the tool shed to feed and clean the doves. He let them out daily and loved to watch them fly, enjoying how high they could go. You could find him almost any time by looking for his silhouette against the bank of cages. He would sometimes attract other boys' doves and hold them for a small ransom. He used to hit me on the back of my head whenever he caught me climbing up to see how the little doves were doing. I wasn't allowed to be up there alone. But Natan did teach me how to tell the male and female doves apart. I wasn't terribly interested in gender at that time, but the ability to distinguish the girl doves from the boy doves taught me something that I hadn't known before.

My next oldest brother, Samuel, was rather different from the rest of us. He showed signs of becoming a businessman from very early on, but he also liked music and pursued it to the extent possible in our town. Since we didn't have a violin in our house, he used the school violin to learn how to play. Samuel also put on theatrical productions in our tool shed. He charged other kids admission and they paid either with buttons that he sold at the market or with pieces of broken glass that he sold to the glass factory. Sometimes they paid with small stones that he put into piles in our backyard and later sold as well. Samuel also liked soccer. All the games were held in the big green meadow not far from the famous old castle. Sometimes we played Jews versus Poles.

Because I was younger, I liked different games. For example, I had a huge metal barrel hoop that I used to push around with a small metal stick and chase. I also made slingshots to shoot stones at birds. I also remember playing by the old synagogue. There was a big pear tree there and we used to pick pears and hide them in piles of hay to make them ripen faster. Sometimes they'd begin to rot, but they were still a delicious treat.

I remember the days when I used to walk to cheder or when I went to the synagogue with my father and couldn't wait for the prayers to end so that I could rush home to taste all the wonderful food that my mother had just cooked. I recall the sweet moments when the whole family used to gather around the dinner table on Fridays for the start of Shabbat (Sabbath) when my mother would light candles, and on Saturday afternoons after synagogue.[7] My mother was a good cook and she enjoyed doing it. I still remember the smell and the taste of her meals. How could I forget her bean stew – her *cholent* – followed by a fruit compote?

Not every child is able to have a good and safe childhood, and I consider myself blessed because those essential formative years were rich with positive and healthy memories and experiences. Rokitno was not a lavish environment, but even something as simple as playing in the mud was fun for me. We weren't a wealthy family but we were strong and loving. Because of that, perhaps mostly because of that, I am alive today. It sustained me through very dark days. Looking back, my childhood and adolescence were wonderful and I now know how irreversible and irretrievable those years are. Even though there was hunger, cold and poverty, I only remember the good things about my family. They are the only things worth preserving.

There was no shame or fear in being a Jewish boy at that time, although there was certainly antisemitism all around us. We felt we

---

7 The Jewish Sabbath, Shabbat, begins on Friday at sundown and ends Saturday at sundown and is ushered in by the lighting of candles.

were a part of Polish society. The antisemitism wasn't masked, but it wasn't always visible either. As a young boy I was familiar with the saying "in every generation they rise up against us to destroy us" that comes from the Haggadah that we read aloud at every Passover seder.[8] But I had no reason to expect that something bad would happen to us. I know now that Rokitno was not paradise, but it was home. I don't actually know why that means so much, but it does. In the hundreds, perhaps thousands, of shtetls – small Jewish towns and villages – across Europe, others shared these feelings. We were part of our families, part of our communities and part of the life around us. We didn't expect to be murdered.

---

8 Passover (in Hebrew, Pesach) is one of the major festivals of the Jewish calendar; it takes place over eight days in the spring and begins with a ritual family meal known as the seder. During the seder, participants read from a book called a Haggadah and recount the story of the Exodus of the Jews from slavery in Egypt. The phrase that Alex Levin quotes here, which refers to the need for Jews to remember their history of persecution and be vigilant, is read from the Haggadah at every seder. For more information, see the glossary.

Our Flight from
the Rokitno Massacre

In August 1939 the Soviet Union and Nazi Germany signed a pact that ensured that the USSR would remain neutral if Germany went to war; in a secret protocol the two countries also divided Poland in the event of a German invasion.[1] On September 1, 1939, Germany invaded Poland from the west. In keeping with the terms of the pact, the Soviet Union invaded from the east on September 17 and soon took control of much of the eastern part of Poland – including my hometown of Rokitno. I vividly remember the Red Army coming in to Rokitno without any resistance from Polish troops and the big red stars on the hats worn by the Red Army soldiers arriving on horseback. Suddenly, the inhabitants of our little shtetl became Soviet citizens.

Everyone had a different perspective on these events. The Jews thought that the Soviets would protect them from the Germans, but the Ukrainians saw the Soviets as occupiers.[2] Many Jews went into the

---

1 The Treaty of Non-Aggression between Germany and the USSR – colloquially known as the Molotov-Ribbentrop Pact – was signed on August 24, 1939. For more information, see the glossary.

2 An independent west Ukrainian republic in Galicia had existed briefly after World War I until the nascent state lost a bitter struggle with the Poles and was incorporated into Poland in 1923. Many Ukrainian nationalists hoped that the outbreak of war between Nazi Germany and the Soviet Union in 1941 would

streets to greet the Red Army troops while we poor children begged the soldiers for tobacco or gathered cigarette butts in hopes of making new cigarettes to sell back to the soldiers.

Soviet doctrine called for replacing religion with political ideology and love of the state. Jewish schools were forced to adopt Soviet curricula and were categorized according to language of instruction – Yiddish, Russian or Ukrainian. Expressions of Jewish nationalism such as speaking Hebrew and promoting Zionism were expressly forbidden, but speaking Yiddish was allowed. The Tarbut high school became a Yiddish school and our Zionist groups were dissolved. People were still permitted to attend synagogue, but any other public displays of religion were banned. Jews whom the Soviets considered rich – such as Shulman, Gitelman and the three Golubovich brothers who owned the woodcutting shop – lost everything. But the Soviets couldn't complete their plans for the Sovietization of Poland.[3] In June 1941 the Nazis broke their pact with the USSR and turned their weapons to the east. The lives of the Ukrainians, the Poles, the Russians and the Jews were never the same.

On June 22, 1941, the Germans invaded the Soviet Union. The Nazis, supported by Ukrainian nationalists, launched a blitzkrieg and within days the train station in Rokitno was bombed. The Red Army retreated and in a flight of panic the Soviet officials in the town caught the last trains going east out of Rokitno. Many ordinary townspeople who could afford horses and carts packed up their belongings and

---

provide an opportunity to re-establish an independent Ukraine. In this context, many Ukrainian nationalists saw the Soviets – who had backed the Poles in crushing Ukrainian independence – as occupiers. When the Nazis invaded eastern Poland in June 1941 many Ukrainian nationalists viewed them as potential liberators and many actively collaborated with German forces.

3 The USSR's policies of "Sovietization" included confiscation, nationalization and redistribution of private and state-owned Polish property, and discrimination against and outright persecution of capitalists and others considered dangerous to the Soviet regime.

headed out as well. Others fled east on foot. The trains were over-crowded with civilians, soldiers, animals and luggage. It was chaos.

Soon after the bombing began Natan came to our house with a horse cart loaded with bread and flour. He tried to convince my father that our whole family should follow him and many others east-ward into the Soviet Union.

"The people who are coming want to kill you, Father," he said with passion. "They will kill every Jewish man, woman and child!"

My father looked at my little brother, Moishe. "They won't kill us." he replied evenly. "They will only keep us in one place, away from the war."

My brother couldn't believe that my father was being so naïve. "Can't you see that they are murderers?!"

"They will not kill us." My father repeated, simply but steadfastly.

"You have heard the stories from the West? You have heard about the Nazis getting rid of the Jews?"

"I don't believe the stories," my father replied. "They are an exag-geration. I don't believe that it would be better to flee. This is our home."

Natan was resolute. "This is not home, Father. No one wants us here. Some of the people in the village are already talking about kill-ing us, talking about hateful acts. Come, pack your things! Come with me to Russia before it's too late."

My father's eyes turned very sad. "You go, Natan. You are young and you can do what you think is best. Your mother and I and the boys will stay here. It is safest for us here."

Based on their experiences during World War 1 when German soldiers had treated Jews kindly, many older people like our father thought that the Germans wouldn't hurt Jews now. In retrospect, such denial was completely misguided. We had heard eyewitness ac-counts from refugees who were fleeing not only Nazi atrocities but also acts of unspeakable cruelty committed by non-Jews from their own communities.

Natan decided without hesitation to head east with our cousins, despite our father's disapproval and the constant air raids. It was the last time I saw Natan until many years after the war.

The rapid withdrawal of the Soviet troops created a legal and political void because German troops and authorities only arrived in Rokitno at the end of July. They were already stationed in nearby Sarny, however, and from there, they put a Ukrainian collaborator named Ratzlav temporarily in charge of a newly-formed band of Ukrainian police in Rokitno. Violence ensued as a wave of antisemitism now rose up in our "little paradise." Polish and Ukrainian collaborators and thieves broke into Jewish homes and robbed them of everything of any value. The violence escalated and Jewish men organized a nightly self-defence patrol armed with axes, shovels and pitchforks. During the first patrol one of these men, Avraham Golod, was stoned to death.

When the Nazis entered the town in August 1941, the Poles and Ukrainians greeted them with ceremonial bread and salt. The Germans introduced their own laws and put Sokolovski, a half-Polish and half-German man from Silesia, in charge of the police force. Denes became commander of the Ukrainische Hilfspolizei, the Ukrainian Auxiliary Police. The head of the town's organized unit of Ukrainian collaborators was a man named Zagorovski.[4]

Desperate and horrifying times started right away as one terrible order followed another. The Nazis established a Jewish ghetto on Stalin Street – my street – and Jews were not allowed to leave the ghetto without special permission.[5] A Judenrat, or Jewish Council, was set

---

4   The Ukrainian Auxiliary Police was formed in the wake of the German occupation of eastern Poland and the Ukraine in June 1941 and actively collaborated with the Nazis in the implementation of their plans to persecute and eventually mass murder Jews. The Ukrainian Auxiliary Police escorted Jews to forced labour sites, guarded the ghettos and engaged in mass-murder shooting operations.

5   Jews were forcibly moved into ghettoes throughout the Nazi's occupied areas in

up to be the spokesmen for the Jewish community and its members were forced to implement the Nazis' vicious and binding orders.[6] The ghetto wasn't sealed with a fence as was the case in other towns, but the Germans and Ukrainians patrolled the perimeter, making it almost impossible to get out. Those who dared to ignore the prohibition, do business with non-Jews or buy or barter their belongings for food were sentenced to immediate execution by shooting.

In compliance with a new order that was issued soon after the ghetto was established, the Nazis, aided by the Ukrainische Hilsfpolizei and Judenrat officials, implemented a twice-daily head count to keep everyone in the ghetto under control and in constant fear. The head count occurred in the market square in the new part of town. The commandant did a roster call and then everyone headed back into the ghetto. Only very young children, the elderly and ill people were exempt from these daily head counts.

Every new order made things worse in the ghetto. Under the threat of death, Jews had to turn in all their gold, silver and furs, as well as their cows and other livestock. More than thirty kilograms of gold were handed over to the Germans as a result of this edict. At the same time, Jews had to report to the police station every day to be assigned to forced labour. Men worked repairing the railroad tracks and roads and in the woodcutting shop. Women worked in the fields. Children ages ten to fourteen were forced to work at the glass factory, and even though I was only nine, I worked there too. All of this was slave labour – we weren't paid any wages. At best, we were given one hundred grams of bread per day.

---

the East. These areas consisted of cramped conditions in a specified and enclosed area of a city or town. For more information, see the glossary.

6 Jewish Councils were established by the Nazis throughout the territories they occupied to facilitate the implementation of their orders. Faced with difficult moral choices, these councils frequently tried to help community members but in fact had no power or independence of action. For more information, see the glossary.

In mid-September 1941, we were forced to make uniforms for the Ukrainian policemen. Their uniforms were made out of black gabardine and if there wasn't enough material provided we had to cut up our own holiday clothing. That was the first time that I saw the Ukrainian trident, the symbol of Ukrainian nationalism, worn by Ukrainians who supported the Nazis because they thought the Nazis would help them gain national independence. There were also many Ukrainians who were committed supporters of Nazism, and not only to further their cause of independence. Ukrainian antisemitism has a more than three-hundred-year-long history that dates back to the seventeenth-century Chmielnicki massacres in which tens of thousands of Jews were murdered in Poland and Ukraine.[7] The twentieth century offered them new opportunities for antisemitic persecution.

My brother Samuel worked for the German officers at the Organization Todt, the German civil and military labour organization.[8] He had to shine the soldiers' boots, split firewood, help their Polish chef cook and serve meals to the officers. Every now and then he'd sneak some food to eat himself and sometimes he was allowed to take home some food scraps and leftovers that had gone bad. Our mother made them into meals by adding oats and wild goosefoot. Samuel later recalled being beaten and humiliated by the Polish chef on a regular basis. One day, when Samuel was polishing the boots of a German officer named Lemel, the officer told him, "If we start killing the Jews, boy, come here and we won't kill you." Samuel realized what was in store for the Jewish community and reported the remark to the Judenrat, which ignored it.

---

7 The Chmielnicki massacre was a massive pogrom against Jews living in the Ukraine that occurred in 1648–1649. It is estimated that three hundred Jewish communities were destroyed and about 100,000 Jews were killed. For more information, see the glossary.

8 The Organization Todt undertook major civilian and military projects under the Nazis and made extensive use of forced and slave labour. For more information, see the glossary.

A month later, in October, 1941, all Jews age ten and older were ordered to wear special patches on their clothing – two yellow circles, each one ten centimetres in diameter with a Star of David in the middle. One was to be worn on the chest, the other one on the back. Jews were not allowed to appear in public without these patches. There were still more prohibitions – for example, Jews were no longer allowed to walk on public sidewalks. In November, SS Captain Ditsch arrived with thirty SS men to take over command of Rokitno and assist in the collection of more "taxes" from the Jews.[9]

Every day spent in the ghetto was filled with nightmares. Food was running out and it was getting harder and harder to get food from the non-Jewish people in the town. People began to die of malnutrition and sickness. We children sometimes managed to sneak out and exchange some clothes for a handful of flour or a piece of bread, but, as I've said, this was a very dangerous mission for all those involved. Risking my life, I managed to sneak out of the ghetto every now and then to trade some of our belongings for bread and eggs. This was dangerous not only for me, but also for the people I bartered with. We lived with constant fear and hunger and the anticipation of death.

These horrors came to a deadly resolution on August 26, 1942. On that day the whole Jewish population of Rokitno was ordered into the market square. No one was exempt now, including infants, the gravely ill and the elderly. Those who couldn't walk were carried to the square on stretchers. Some people carried others on their backs. German soldiers and German and Ukrainian police surrounded the square. They began by separating children, women, men and the elderly. The situation developed into fear and disorder. Soon, deafening screams and moans filled the square. People panicked. Children were clinging to their mothers. Everyone was trying to defend the old and the sick.

---

9 SS is the abbreviation for Schutzstaffel (Protective Force). For more information, see the glossary.

All of a sudden, a sharp scream pierced the air: "Jews, they're going to kill us all now." It was Mindl Eisenberg, a big, tall, brave woman nicknamed "The Cossack" who saw the police squadron arrive from behind the train station and alerted the crowd. Anguished, people began to run for their lives. Men ran to find their wives and children. Everyone was trying to escape. Only bullets could stop them. The guards fired at the crowd and dozens of people were killed instantly, covering the square with blood. In this hell, my seventeen-year-old brother, Samuel, found me, grabbed me by the arm and we started running....

That was the last time we saw our mother, our father and our five-year-old brother, Moishe. We found out later that our father had been captured with other survivors of the shooting in the market square and taken to the Sarny area, approximately forty kilometres from Rokitno. Just outside of Sarny, in the ravines by the brick factory, he was shot along with some 18,000 other Jews who met horrifying deaths in that awful place. Witness accounts of the massacre say that the ground, covered with hundreds of bodies, was moving for days because people had been buried alive.[10]

We never found out exactly what happened to our mother and our youngest brother.

My brother and I ran away from the market square to the house

---

10 The Sarny massacre took place on August 27, 1942, the day after the massacre in Rokitno. In Rokitno, the murders in the town square were carried out by a combination of Ukrainian and German police. Between one and three hundred Jews were killed on the spot and the remaining 800 to 1,200 – except for those who, like Alex and Samuel Levin, managed to escape – were forced onto railway cattle cars and taken to nearby Sarny, where they were shot along with thousands of other Jews and at least one hundred Roma who had also been gathered there from around the district. In Sarny, German and Ukrainian policemen, assisted by some two hundred members of the Organization Todt, murdered more than 18,000 people.

of the German officer who had promised to save Samuel. We broke into the house through the back window, but unhappily encountered the Polish chef. Without hesitation, my brother took my hand and we ran out the door into the backyard and then through the yard toward the woods. We crawled underneath the rail cars that had, I know now, been prepared for transporting Jews to the Sarny area and escaped into the forest. We ran as fast as we could and kept on running.

We managed to escape Rokitno. We didn't know where to go at first, but soon headed deep into the woods. We wanted to get as far away from that murderous place as possible. The forest was dense and thick and frightening for two boys already deeply traumatized, but we soon found some small relief. In the woods we came across other escapees. At first we met one person and then a few more until there were a significant number of us together in the woods. The adults talked to each other in whispers.

"Where is your family?" one woman asked. Samuel shook his head. "I don't know. Back there, in the village. We had to run."

"We can't go back, not for any reason. They are killing everybody, women and children." One woman had two children with her. "My husband fell behind me. He was shot. I couldn't go back because of the children. What are we supposed to do?" There were brief stories of anguish and fear. "They will come after us, too!" someone said. There was hurried discussion among the adults. Finally, they agreed. "We're in more danger if we all stay together," they said. "Let's break up into small groups. That way it will be harder to find us."

For the next two weeks or so, Samuel and I wandered alone, moving toward the Polish villages of Netreba and Okopy. The woods in that area were denser and the swamps there provided better cover. I remember occasionally meeting people along the way who warned us that we should only go into the villages in the case of extreme emergency. If we did come close to any villages, they said, we should still stay as close to the woods as possible in case we ran into the police. But it wasn't only the police that we had to worry about – even the ordinary local citizens sometimes greeted Jews with axes and pitch-forks, and we were told that the Nazis were offering one kilo of salt for every Jew the locals turned in. When we did go to try to find or beg for food we mostly went into the Polish villages because they were more generous to us than the Ukrainians were.

Our journey over those couple of weeks was very hard and dangerous, but there were some memorable acts of kindness and courage that stand out. The two names in particular that are forever etched into my heart are Ludwik Wrodarczyk, a Polish Catholic priest, and Felicia Masojada, a Polish teacher from Okopy. When we arrived at their door after the massacre in Rokitno, they hid us in a closet and gave us some clothes and enough food to last a little while. We found out later that these wonderful people, truly good souls, paid a high price for their compassion – they were executed by Ukrainian Nazi collaborators. Many witnesses have since written about the lives of these remarkable people in such accounts as "There Were Three of Them" by Yanek Bronislav, a retired Polish army colonel, and "My Volynski Epos" by Leon Zhur. Wrodarczyk and Masojada's courage and commitment to humanity set a shining example for younger generations. In 1998, Samuel and I initiated the process to have Wrodarczyk and Masojada declared Righteous Among the Nations by the Jewish Holocaust memorial organization Yad Vashem in Jerusalem. The presentation was made in 2000.

During this time we ended up staying for a while at a farm belonging to a Polish peasant. He fed us and in return we had to work for him. Samuel was assigned various household tasks and from 4:00 a.m. until late at night I had to tend to the cattle grazing in the woods. There were eleven cows. The peasant was afraid that the Germans, gangs of Ukrainian bandits or Soviet partisans would take away his cows, and so he would give me a slice of bread and some lard and ask me to take the cows deep into the woods. Later on, we hid the cows in makeshift shacks in the forest. The woods had their own complicated underground life – along with Jewish refugees and different groups of partisans, they were also inhabited by Ukrainian bandits who hated Germans, Soviets and Jews.

We didn't stay at this Polish peasant's farm for long. It wasn't long before there weren't any local people who were willing to give us even temporary shelter anymore. It was too dangerous for them. Lost and without any place to go, separated from other Jews who were also hiding in the woods, Samuel and I decided to return to Rokitno. On our way back, we watched through the trees as people looted empty Jewish houses, searching for anything valuable that might have been left behind. They used axes to cut into the walls to look for hidden gold and valuables. Before the massacres in Rokitno and Sarny, these people hadn't stood up for the Jews, hadn't tried to help them. After their cruel deaths, they robbed them.

In this case – unlike my memories of my family and childhood – the evil is easier to remember than the good. In his book, Victor Polischuk writes, "I'm ashamed of what my countrymen did during the war. I'm ashamed of those who led the Jews to their deaths. I knew them. I still know them, these nationalists. I saw them kill. I know what they're capable of." [11]

At some point we came upon a small caravan of horse carts. The people saw us, two frightened boys, and called us over. When they found out that we were Jewish and were heading back to Rokitno, they said in Ukrainian, "What are you talking about, boys? You have to run deep into the woods – the Germans are still killing all the Jews."

This chance encounter reignited our desire to survive and we escaped back into the woods. Along the way we ran into many other Jewish escapees and refugees. But we remembered to stay in very small groups. Every night after dark, we would crawl cautiously into stacks of hay in the fields, covering ourselves so that the only opening was a small breathing hole. We sometimes secretly spent the night in

---

11 Victor Polischuk, *Bitter Truth* (Toronto, Warsaw & Kiev, 1995), in Ukrainian.

a tool shed. No matter what the circumstances, we were always terrified that we might be caught.

My brother and I decided to look for a group of partisans to join. We knew that there were communist "Red" partisans – whose activities were actively coordinated by the Soviet government – and Polish partisans, as well as a Ukrainian group who had their own horses and uniforms with a special emblem. We finally met up with a group of Polish partisans in a village – members of the Armia Krajowa, or Home Army – and asked to become members, but they only wanted Samuel so we didn't join them.[12]

We continued our journey through the woods searching for partisans, looking now for Soviet partisans. We found them but they didn't want to take on Jews. At that point we were near the village of Karpilovka. The partisans there warned us that the villagers had recently killed a couple of Jewish boys with axes. That made us seek refuge further away, again near the villages of Netreba and Okopy that were populated primarily by Poles who were themselves being attacked and killed by Ukrainian nationalists. But as much as possible, we made sure to stay hidden in the woods.

---

12 Formed in February 1942, the Armia Krajowa (AK, or Home Army) was the largest Polish resistance movement in German-occupied Poland in World War II. For more information, see the glossary.

We Take Shelter in the Forest

One night, after Samuel and I had been wandering for about two weeks, living hand to mouth, we saw a small campfire in the woods. When we approached it carefully we found a group of Jews we knew from Rokitno – Rachel Wasserman, Rachel's two children, Bluma and Taibele, and her sister Dosya, Dvoshil Svetchnik with her son, Haim, and daughter, Henya, Shmuel Bagel, Avraham Eisenberg and Todres Linn.

The feeling of safety that we found in our reunion was brief. That night we were awoken by noises and saw three armed men standing in front of us. They introduced themselves as partisans, gave us food and left. The next night they came back and said they could take one woman to help them out. Dosya volunteered. But we'd been deceived – we soon found out that they were actually bandits. We never learned what happened to Dosya.

This event made us really understand how desperate our circumstances were. We couldn't go back to any civilized place and it was now getting cold and we would soon be in real danger of freezing to death. We were frightened and desperate and yet within each of us was a flicker of purpose, a determination to survive whatever might come. Motivated by fierce emotions we were unable to comprehend, we went deeper into the woods.

I don't remember how it happened, who might have made the decisions, but a group of us started working together. If that hadn't happened I'm sure that Samuel and I would have died. I don't remember how the plan took shape, but we began to make a shelter in the middle of the woods, far from the perimeter where it might be found. It was a crude dugout that was to be shared by ten people – Samuel and me; Dvoshil Svetchnik, her son, Haim, (now Haim Bar Or) and her daughter, Henya; Rachel Wasserman and her two daughters, Bluma and Taibele; and Gitl Gamulka and her son Lova (now Larry).

Both adults and children helped make this ramshackle structure; each of us contributed what we could. We began by digging a deep hole in the soil and reinforcing it with wood and bark around the sides and edges, which we built up slightly above ground level. Over the hole, which we came to call "the cave," we piled branches and sticks over the top to form a roof that would both serve as camouflage and protect us. We were careful to make the dugout look like a natural outcrop of bushes.

Around the sides on the inside of the dugout were crude bunk beds for sleeping. We built a simple but effective fireplace in the centre of our hiding space and left an opening above it to allow the smoke to escape. We only burned oak since it gave off little smoke; fortunately the forest was very rich in old oak trees. We dug a small well just outside the cave to provide us with pure water.

We called ourselves "the forest Jews." It was an affectionate name, something that gave us a feeling of family and togetherness. This dugout became our home. We disguised it as well as we could – in fact it was sometimes even hard for us to find it when we returned from looking for food. An unusual oak with a branch bent in a particular way served as our only marker.

Our days passed with difficulty, mostly because of our fear of being caught but also, most immediately, because of the ever-present reality of hunger. Even in this seeming chaos, however, we established some sense of routine. We would approach the outskirts of a village, see a light in a window and beg for food. We never went into the centre of a village. Our days were focused on getting food and not getting caught. We were always looking for ways to fill our stomachs. Sometimes we looked for metal cans that we could turn into lanterns to scare away wolves. We looked out for police, horses and Germans. Sometimes we'd see tire tracks from a car.

Under less desperate circumstances, living in the woods might have been an adventure, but there was no sense of adventure for us in any of this. We had lost our parents, and now hunger and death followed us constantly. We had to find wood, mushrooms, whatever food we could. We kept having to go farther and farther away from our cave to find what we needed.

Because we knew it was a matter of pure survival, we felt no guilt at stealing what we needed. To get beets, turnips or potatoes from farmers' fields in winter we had to dig though the frozen ground. We learned from the wild boars how to steal potatoes without leaving any trace that people had been there. We ate the white beets and turnips that farmers grew to feed to the barn animals, digging them up from the ground or stealing them from the storage sheds. Day after day went on like this. We always had to find food. There was never enough food. I have never forgotten what it means to be so hungry.

We had no idea what was going on in the outside world. We didn't have access to any information – no newspapers, no electricity, no radio. But the most important thing is that we two orphans adapted to life in the wild and survived.

By the time a year had passed, our situation had somewhat improved. Although our lives were still fraught with danger and hunger, the forest became more and more our home. We had learned more and more skills that helped us survive and made us that smallest bit more comfortable. Despite the odds, we hadn't been caught. We became more secure and hopeful, extremely resourceful and clever. Survival was not a game for us but an earnest pursuit.

We learned how to make moccasins out of oak bark steamed over the fire. Instead of socks we wrapped our feet in sacks that the peasants used to separate the buttermilk from sour clotted milk to make cottage cheese. We stole these sacks during our nightly missions, ate the cheese and used the cloth. In winter we wrapped our feet in *volosin*, a very thin and soft but warm material woven from dried hay. We learned how to use the riches of the forest to survive. We learned to identify which mushrooms and berries were poisonous and which ones were good. We picked blackberries, blueberries, cranberries and raspberries. We learned to tap birch trees for a bittersweet-tasting syrup and made cups out of birch bark to catch the sap. Sometimes my brother even managed to get some wild honey from beehives.

We were always aware of the very real dangers around us, but in addition to them, we forest wanderers were tormented by another scourge – the terrible and incessant lice. They were large and insatiable. We had them not only in our hair but under our armpits and in our groins – they crawled everywhere. The worst thing about them was the constant itching that kept us awake at night. But the forest also taught us how to get rid of them: we stripped naked and buried our clothes in anthills. The ants ate the lice and their nits. We weren't as successful in avoiding another plague – an awful rash that spread from between our toes all over our bodies to our arms, legs, chest and even our buttocks.

Other vivid, fearful and even painful memories of our time in the forest have long stayed with me. The screams of owls, like human screams, pursued us at night. They seemed almost mystical because they were ever-present, but also, in a sense, invisible. I can still hear the sound of howling wolves and see their glittering eyes following us as they looked for prey. I remember frequent encounters with foxes and with swamp snakes when we collected tall oak samplings.

Death, too, was a real part of our life in the forest. We had to bury two people in our group. In the fall of 1942, death came for Haim's mother, Dvoshil, and his sister, Henya. Dvoshil leaned on my brother's shoulder to sleep one night and by morning she had frozen to death. Soon her daughter Henya died as well. They both died of malnutrition and hypothermia, their bodies grey and swollen, their skin cracked. We buried them in a state of shock without any real ceremony. These nightmarish images still haunt me. Seeing these members of our group perish slowly was a very profound experience for a little boy of ten. The tragedy of what I had witnessed was almost too much to bear. I was more than frightened – I was literally dumbstruck and remained silent for a long time after these deaths.

"Everything passes – and childhood, and the fairytales of the woods…. Everything passes, alas, and only the grey wolves – oh, ever so immortal – greet us along the way." These words of the poet Naum Sagalovsky describe very well our life and struggle during that time. Some of what it was like in the forest is also expressed in a poem written by a friend of mine, Fred Zolotkovsky, when he visited Rokitno with me many years later:

These dark woods are our salvation.
Knee deep in water, yet we are alive!
Dreams preserve us.
Our dugout is the sweetest home.
Our only hope that Germans don't rush in
All at once with a pack of dogs,
That police won't notice with trained eyes
Smoke rising through the darkness.
We all are worth only a carton of salt.
One kilogram is the price for your whole life:
Your soul, and heart, and blood
And only because you are a Jew.

In December 1943, after almost eighteen months in the forest, hope began to light our way. The tide of the war had turned and the Red Army was pushing the Nazis westward. We started to hear promising sounds of battle approaching in the distance and we began to hope for liberation. Now when we went to look for food the villagers were a bit friendlier toward us. They wanted to look good when the Soviets arrived. They certainly didn't want to appear as if they had collaborated with the Nazis.

But with hope came other emotions too powerful to describe. With time and distance it is easy to make generalizations about the war and the behaviour of those who were involved in it. It's much harder to grapple with questions about the meaning of our survival, the relationship between the Jews and the Poles and the Ukrainians, the role that partisans and bandits played in this conflict. One thing I'm sure of is that the few of us who survived didn't do so because we were smart or skilful – we were, quite plainly, lucky. Survival wasn't a matter of personal success or failure – we didn't survive by our wits alone while millions of others perished.

To the reader who asks why our families didn't resist the Nazis, I ask in return, was it possible to resist the Nazis? We didn't know how to deal with forces that were so much greater than us and about which we knew so little. My own father didn't believe what was coming, even when confronted with eyewitness accounts. Such horror and brutality was inconceivable and we didn't understand it. Who knew at that time that such evil and hatred could exist?

In the end, I want young people to know that we children managed to live in the woods in isolation for a year and a half, sentenced to death by the Nazis, and we survived. I can't say for sure how it was that we survived. Who saved us? When people ask me if I believe in God, I say that my God is the forest. I was saved by the forest, so if God made the forest, then I believe in God. But if God was very close to me now, I would ask him, "Why did you allow them to kill my brother and my mother and my father? Where were you during all that suffering?"

A child may not have a mature understanding of God. He or she may only think of God as a benevolent being who makes things happen. But a child understands good and evil. Without knowing it, my belief in the possibility of a force for good faded away. My belief in God as a protective creator, the God I had been taught about as a child, burst like a balloon. Nonetheless, my identity as a Jew remained very real and very strong.

A little boy needs to find order and purpose in something. For me, the forest served that purpose. The woods gave us what we needed, gave us life and took it away. In the fertile soil of Polesie, the forest was remarkable. Thousand-year-old oaks intertwined with hundred-year-old pines. We sought protection in those woods. They were our refuge and our hearth. Every tree became a fortress. Every shrub was a fort. The forest became our best friend. I am sorry that I am not a poet or a songwriter who could find the words I can't to praise the forest as my saviour and my faithful benefactor. The forest saved us.

Out of the Woods

After living in the woods for a year and a half without showers or new clothes we were filthy, exhausted and ravenously hungry. Soon we began hearing artillery noises nearby. That was a very good thing as it meant that the Germans were retreating. The Red and Polish partisans became more active and it became easier to get food. Although we had a general idea about what was going on we were ignorant of the specifics. There were no radios anywhere. Information was sparse.

Finally, on January 6, 1944, the Red Army liberated Rokitno and began to pursue the Nazis to the west. Those of us who had survived were like wounded animals; we had a hard time adjusting to the idea that we'd have to leave the forest. Our daily sufferings had created a bond between us in the depths of the Polesie woods.

We had learned to live in the safety of the woods, but now we had to learn the horrible reality of our family and community's fate. We left our dugout home in the woods and headed into the unknown. Exhausted and ragged, we went back to the places where our childhood, our schooling, and our incredible suffering had begun. When Samuel and I and some other survivors finally gathered in Rokitno, we numbered only thirty people. We were all in shock when we learned how desperately our Jewish community had been ravaged.

My brother and I heard the truth about our family's tragic fate and then went to visit the only people we knew in town, the Polish Wrublevski family. Our families used to be friends and as children we were sometimes invited to celebrate New Year's at their house and pick candy off the Christmas tree. Now, under the circumstances, they were as kind as they could be. They gave us food and some clothing and let us spend the night.

Early the next morning we went into the centre of town, where we met a Red Army sergeant-major named Gurinovich. He asked us what had happened in our town. After we told him the whole story he suggested that Samuel join a local field unit as a brigade volunteer. And as soon as he made sure that I would have a place as well, that's what he did.

The sergeant-major took me to Boris Markovich Krupkin, who was in charge of Red Army field hospital No. 2408 of the 13th Army of the First Ukrainian Front.[1] A short, stout man with a wide forehead, Krupkin listened to the sergeant-major's retelling of our story and ordered that I be taken to the army bathhouse immediately and washed and clothed with a suitable uniform until my own fitted uniform was ready. That's how I became the so-called "son of the regiment," a recruit of the field hospital and officially an orphan.[2] I was eleven years old.

From the very first day everyone from the head of the field hospital to the head of the field pharmacy treated me with warmth and caring. My duties started right away and included helping out in the field pharmacy and the mailroom. I assisted with measuring the dos-

---

1 In Soviet military parlance, a "front" was a large, coordinated group of field armies that could be self-sufficient for long periods of time and was responsible for a large geographic area. Usually commanded by a full general, a front is akin to a Western "army group." For more information on the First Ukrainian Front, see the glossary.

2 The designation of "son of the regiment" was given to the orphaned boys picked up by the Red Army who served in uniform.

age of powders and potions, and also delivered mail to the wounded soldiers and officers.

This was the beginning of a new chapter in my life, that of an orphan in uniform under the watchful eye of an entire military base. I became their favourite. They were all amazed at a young child's instinctive resistance to the horrors of war. They all wanted to share their love with me and save me from further harm. I made new friends every day, but inside I wanted to be fighting at the front. Even in those early years I had hopes of avenging my family.

The Red Army was rapidly advancing westward, defeating the Nazis, but not without casualties of their own. We could tell the difficulty, scale and success of any front mission by the number of wounded we received at the hospital. It was here that I began to understand the realities of war and its consequences. I saw with my own eyes all the wounded soldiers and officers. I can still hear them screaming. I can still see the bloody bandages, made quickly in the overcrowded emergency room. I can still smell the rotting wounds. It haunts me to this day.

Even though the field hospital was located fairly far from the front lines, it was still subject to German air raids. I vividly recall one such raid in the town of Dubno when I was in the cranial-facial unit of the hospital. The head of the pharmacy and I were carrying medicine to the wounded when the bomb hit and the shockwave smashed us against the wall. It was the first time I had personally experienced such a powerful physical force. I only suffered minor injuries but my memory of it cannot be erased. There were many casualties in the cranial-facial unit because the bomb directly hit a corner of the building.

The people who worked at the mobile field hospital were courageous, sensitive and honest people. There were people of many different nationalities among the staff, all united in the name of fighting the Nazis. Most of the doctors and administrators were Jewish, however, and I knew that at least one of them had personally suffered at the hands of the Germans. I was able to speak to some of these people in Yiddish, but mostly I communicated in very broken Russian that I only began to pick up slowly.

Neither air raids nor artillery strikes could stop the medical personnel from their mission. Sometimes they performed surgeries without electricity by the light of kerosene lamps. A husband and wife by the name of Gurevich were in charge of the X-ray machine and were always ready to assist the surgical team. They were from Moscow and when the field hospital passed through the town of Brody, they had adopted a Jewish boy named Misha. He moved with them to Moscow after the war and I later visited them there. Although destiny has parted our ways since then, these heroic people are forever in my memory.

It is also impossible to forget our commissar, Zhiharevich, a middle-aged woman who always wore a leather jacket and a revolver on her belt.[3] She spent a great deal of time with the wounded, cheering them up and loudly announcing whenever I brought the mail, "Here is Shurik with a message from home!"[4] The atmosphere of anticipation and joy of the soldiers at that moment was indescribable.

I also remember a doctor named Maya Naumovna Suhuvolskaya, a young woman of medium complexion with short black hair. Her white uniform was always stained with blood from previous surgeries. This courageous woman was very motherly toward me and always found time to ask about my past and my dreams of the future. She told me about her parents in the town of Kyrgyztorg in the Kyrgyzstan Soviet Republic and about her post-war dreams. She wanted to marry an artillery battery captain she had met at the front and adopt me as her son. Life, however, dictates its own story. Maya

---

3 A commissar was an official of the Communist Party who was assigned to teach party principles and ensure party loyalty in a Soviet military unit. For more information, see the glossary.

4 Shurik is a common Russian nickname for Alexander.

Naumovna's love for the officer ended tragically when he was killed shortly before the end of the war. I don't know anything about her post-war destiny. The stories of tragedy and strength outnumber even those of hatred. These are just a few of the people with whom I shared joy and sorrow.

Our hospital was part of the 13th Army under the command of General Pukhov. The mobile field hospital and its entire staff followed the first echelon of troops. As the Red Army advanced and seized major strategic locations, we learned more and more about the Nazis' cruelties. My first encounter with the horrors of the Nazi camps happened when we got to the Polish town of Rzeszów.[5] We met with many witnesses and survivors and they told us their horrible stories. The soldiers who took care of me wanted to protect me from these tales, but a strong desire for revenge was growing inside of me. I wanted to avenge the deaths of my relatives and my people and decided that I would become a professional military man.

By the end of July 1944 we were already in central Poland. The Red Army crossed the Vistula river and liberated the town of Sandomierz, where I finally met up with my brother Samuel who had been travelling with the Red Army as a brigade volunteer. We talked about our family, about relatives who might still be in the Soviet Union, and especially about our brother Natan who had retreated with the Soviet troops at the beginning of the war. And according to our mother, our only aunt, her sister, Roza Vainer, had gone to Birobidzhan in the USSR with her husband in 1933 to help build the Jewish Autonomous Region there.[6] We remembered that the day the Soviet troops entered

---

5 The Nazis operated ten forced labour camps in and around Rzeszów, and the town was also not far from the murder camp at Belzec where most Jews from the region were killed in 1942 and 1943.

6 The Jewish Autonomous Region, located in the far eastern part of the USSR, close to the Chinese border, was established by Stalin in 1934 as part of the Soviet Nationalities Policy, which proposed that each national group in the Soviet Union

Rokitno in September 1939, our mother couldn't stop talking about her sister. While we were together, Samuel and I prepared and mailed a care package to Aunt Roza in Birobidzhan.

Soviet troops were already successfully fighting the Nazis in other countries as well. During the liberation of Poland, I saw Germans who had been taken by the Soviets as prisoners of war (POWs). They were no longer the macho soldiers who used to pose for photos beside murdered Jews. Soviet soldiers commonly attended, witnessed and participated in the executions of the German POWs who had been convicted of war crimes by the Soviet army. In stark contrast, I also saw people walking along the roads with baby strollers trying to build new lives after returning to their homes in towns and villages that had been liberated. These were people who had escaped death in the concentration camps and labour camps because the Germans ran out of time. I still cannot fathom how mankind allowed such a horror to take place. When I consider everything I witnessed, I think it more than any person, let alone a child, should witness, but somehow I remained normal. This is something that remains a mystery.

Every person who lived through the war, every citizen of the Soviet Union, from children to the elderly, remembers the characteristic radio signals and the unforgettable voice of the radio announcer Yuri Levitan who always began his broadcast with the words: "Moscow is speaking." And one broadcast that none of us will ever forget was when he said: "Here is the latest update from the Soviet Information Bureau (Sovinformburo): The troops of the First Ukrainian Front have successfully crossed the river Oder…." With this announcement it was official – Soviet troops had entered Germany and had begun to defeat the Nazis on their own turf. In their wake, our field hospital

---

receive a territory in which to pursue cultural autonomy within a socialist framework. By 1939, over 17,000 Jews lived in the region. The town of Birobidzhan was its administrative centre. For more information, see the glossary.

also entered Germany. Close to the front lines, I saw the consequences of the war over and over again.

As the Red Army entered Eastern Prussia, more than two million Germans fled westward. They were German refugees fleeing from the advance of the Soviets and the certain punishment they would receive for the cruelties committed by their fellow citizens. And indeed, I witnessed the behaviour of the Soviet army on their victorious march through German territory – and it wasn't virtuous. I remember seeing a woman who was bleeding from a knife wound inflicted by some Soviet soldier asking for help. No one helped her. Rapes were very common too. Soviet officers would mark the outside of houses where rapes were being committed with a coded message: "The house is mined, Senior Sergeant Ivanov."

In Germany, I saw my brother Samuel more often. I became friends with other recruits of nearby regiments and together we raided German houses for clocks, watches and other trophies to send to surviving relatives back home. My brother got the idea to start sending such packages to Aunt Roza in Birobidzhan. We put small pieces of gold and other small but valuable items into bars of soap by cutting the soap in half, making a hole in the middle, inserting the item, and putting the two pieces of soap seamlessly back together. This was necessary because the packages were often opened and the valuables lost or stolen. We didn't find out until much later that our aunt bartered these valuable packages in exchange for bread and other food because by then she was a widow with an infant to feed. She didn't know that the cheap soap we sent her was actually so valuable.

By March 1945 the German army was losing one battle after another and began drafting all young men born from 1929 on. It was Germany's last gasp. The Third Reich was sinking. Just at this time, as victory was imminent, Stalin issued an order that all adolescent military recruits who had been picked up on the Red Army's journey westward were to be sent back to the home front and placed in orphanages or schools so they could continue their education. All these children, myself included, had already graduated from the hardest lessons of life, but now we would have a chance to get a proper secondary education and perhaps begin to experience normal youthful lives. This order was issued in April 1945, when I had just turned thirteen. It also marked the beginning of a thirty-year separation from my brother Samuel.

On the day of my departure for Moscow my brother handed me a small suitcase with a few things that I might need. I already had a pocketknife and a small pistol hidden in my gear. A pregnant nurse who was going home to Schelkovo in the Moscow region escorted me. Together we started our journey on eastbound freight trains loaded with technical equipment from dismantled German factories.[7]

In Belarus we stopped in a village where the nurse's parents lived. There I witnessed a common post-war tragedy on the home front. A bunch of kids found a blasting cartridge, a live bomb that weighed two hundred grams, and decided to detonate it in the water to kill fish. They asked me to join them, but I knew the danger. I tried everything I could to warn them, but they were reckless and wouldn't listen. While I was standing in the distance a terrible explosion rocked the lake. One boy died and another boy was severely wounded in the blast.

Saddened, my companion and I left the village and headed for Moscow. A new world was opening up in front of me and I adjusted quickly, as only a child can. Moscow was beautiful and an enormous surprise but, used to surprises by this time, the urban environment

---

7 As the USSR occupied Germany in 1945, it embarked on a policy geared toward economic compensation and the rehabilitation of its own economy, as well as punishing Germany: whole factories were systematically dismantled and shipped back to the USSR. This is the equipment that Alex accompanied eastward in the early summer of 1945. The post-war settlement agreed upon at the Potsdam Conference in 1946 included this policy of "demontage" as part of a general reparations plan to exact compensation for the physical damage wrought by Germany abroad.

didn't overwhelm me. In some ways, it didn't seem so imposing – it was almost like another kind of forest to be explored and reckoned with.

The nurse left me at a halfway house for recovering soldiers who were en route back to the front lines. The centre was larger, with many people living and working there. This makeshift residence was at 32 Stromynka Street, not far from the Yauza river. Since I was an enlisted army recruit I was eligible for the standard army allowances including food, clothing and money. With each passing day more and more orphans came to Moscow, so more young recruits arrived at the house.

I kept dreaming of a military career. I wanted to avenge the innocent people who had been murdered, to save them from further dehumanization. But the administration of the halfway house had plans to enroll us all into different trade schools. Because of this, I decided to run away from the halfway house and when I did, I luckily encountered an army man, Captain Musihin, a commander of the local infantry unit (OMSR 86). He took a great liking to me, enlisted me in his brigade and decided that he would help me pursue my dream: to become a cadet at one of the Suvorov Military Schools that was located in Voronezh in southwestern Russia.[8] Once again I had been lucky enough to meet a kind, sensitive stranger. Not only did he enlist me, but he also asked his wife, who was a teacher, to help me improve my Russian.

I approached my studies with great enthusiasm and still found time to explore Moscow. I went to the movies (which were free for

---

8 Created in 1943, the Suvorov Military Schools were a group of boarding schools for boys aged fourteen to seventeen that taught military-related subjects as well as a general high school curriculum. The boarding aspect of the schools was an important element because they enrolled a great many war orphans and children of single mothers. The schools became very prestigious in the USSR and were soon seen as the best way to start a career as an officer. For more information, see the glossary.

those who had returned from the front lines). I was in Moscow on the joyous day World War ii ended. On the radio, Levitan's powerful voice praised the people for their great victory. The streets of Moscow were overflowing with joy. People everywhere were dancing and crying. Everyone was hugging and kissing each other. As a young man in a uniform, I couldn't take a step without people kissing me, giving me treats or inviting me into their homes. On May 9, 1945, a victory parade took place in the Red Square and sealed this chapter in the history of mankind. It was an amazing experience, but the memory of it did wear off in time. My memories of the war itself, by contrast, have lasted a lifetime.

After the celebrations, I began to concentrate on getting into the Suvorov Military School. Following Musihin's advice, I went to the Jewish Anti-Fascist Committee in Kropotkin Street, where I met another great man – the head of the committee himself – Solomon Mihailovich Mikhoels.[9] He instructed his staff to prepare a letter of recommendation for the Suvorov Military School on my behalf. The office of the military schools was very close to Kropotkin Street.

Mikhoels also gave me a season pass to the Jewish Theatre and I soon became a regular. As a result of my visit to the Jewish Anti-Fascist Committee I met a journalist who asked me for an interview about my life. He wrote an article titled "Khaver Royterarmeyer" (Comrade Soldier of the Red Army) that was published in the committee's Yiddish-language newspaper *Eynikayt* (Unity).[10] The Jewish

---

9 The Jewish Anti-Fascist Committee was established by Soviet authorities in April 1942 to help drum up political and material support for the Soviet struggle against Nazi Germany from the Jewish communities in the West. Solomon Mikhoels, the popular actor and director of the Moscow Jewish State Theatre, was appointed chairman, and many well-known Soviet Jews participated in the committee's activities. For more information, see the glossary.

10 Alex Levin's translation of the Yiddish article is included in the appendices on page 122.

Anti-Fascist Committee was very influential at this time. In the spring and summer of 1943, the organization had sent Mikhoels and Itsik Feffer, a Yiddish poet, to speak to Jewish audiences in the United States, Canada and Mexico to rally Jewish support for Stalin and the Soviet Union.

My Moscow saga didn't very last long because after just a few weeks I was called in to take the entrance examinations to the Suvorov Military School. At one point I had to write a Russian-language dictation. I can't begin to tell you how nervous I was – I had only just begun studying Russian formally with Captain Musihin's wife and my Russian was at best mediocre. But even though I made many mistakes, I was accepted. I ran to tell Musihin my news and by September 28, 1945, it was official, I was no longer receiving allowances from his brigade.

The Suvorov Military School

I ask of my progeny to follow my example.

ALEXANDER VASILYEVICH SUVOROV

On a clear September day in 1945 I received my travel allowance and went to the Moscow train station to wait for my train to Voronezh. The station was crowded and there were other children who were also travelling to Voronezh. Sitting on a bench, I looked around anxiously and wondered what awaited me at the Suvorov Military School. How would I manage with such poor knowledge of Russian? The future was unclear and the uncertainty scared me.

My contemplation was interrupted by a woman who noticed me sitting alone. Her name was Tamara Akimovna Sidorova. Her son, Novik Sidorov, was also waiting to board the train for the cadet school in Voronezh and he later became one of my best friends. Tamara Sidorova was a middle-aged woman with an unusual but very beautiful appearance. Her voice was soft and warm. I felt comfortable telling her my life story, rich as it was with love, luck, horror and insight for one so young. She listened to me attentively, stroking my thick black hair. When I was finished, she told her son to befriend me and invited me to spend my holidays with their family in Moscow.

The train came and we soon departed. My nervousness grew with every clinking sound made by the swiftly revolving train wheels. But

Novik and I soon began to have fun with the other boys who were travelling in the same rail car. We stayed close together as Novik's mother had requested. The journey was long – more than twenty-four hours – and we had to sleep on bare cots without any bedding. Despite the fact that the war was over, the trains were still full of soldiers, mostly those who had just recovered from injuries and were now travelling home. Most of the civilians on the train were women, often with infants. The rail cars were overcrowded and reeked of sweat. Future Suvorov cadets occupied almost half the rail cars. These were boys who had survived the horrors of war – air raids and artillery attacks, famine and cold. Vadim Mihanovsky described their experience in one of his poems:

> And I remember without effort
> How we were bombed in '41,
> How the train station covered the people
> With the debris, bricks and dust.
> I won't forget the fighter jets
> Gunning down through the train roofs,
> And how the children cried in those rail cars
> Clinging to their dead mothers.[1]

But there were no other Jews who, like me, had survived an entirely other set of horrors in Poland.

The train wheels carried on with their melody. As the boys got acquainted, everyone shared stories of their childhood years. Everyone tried to look older than his actual age in hopes of becoming a leader of the pack. Novik was the only one I came to trust on that train and I continued to do so for many years following that journey. Indeed, his loyalty toward me was first tested on that trip. Our conversation was

---

1 From Vadim Mihanovsky and L. Bergelson, *Memory* (Voronezh-Novosibirsk, 2001), a collection of thirteen poems in Russian.

interrupted by a comment from a boy who seemed older than us because he was taller. He insulted the Jewish people by using the derog-
atory Russian word *zhid*. Before I had a chance to say anything, my
friend Novik lunged forward and grabbed him with every intention
of throwing him off the moving train. Taken aback, Victor changed
his tone and apologized.

Among all the boys in the rail car, I was the only one with a real
military uniform. This sparked everyone's interest and respect – they
saw it as a symbol of my experience and maturity, and also of the
great victory of the USSR. The boys crowded the uncomfortable cots
and enthusiastically asked me questions about what it was like at the
front. Most of them had lost their fathers in the war, but some of their
fathers were still serving in the Red Army.

We finally arrived at the Voronezh train station. Our common
nervousness grew with each passing moment. The officer who was
assigned to escort us to the Suvorov Military School was a very experienced fatherly man who had also taken good care of us during
the train journey. We were all put into the back of a large truck and
driven to Pridacha, a suburb of Voronezh. The road from the train
station to the school wasn't long, but it was long enough to notice
the battle scars. Voronezh had suffered greatly during the battles for
liberation.[2]

After we passed Petrovsky Park, which would later become the
focal point of many important moments in my life, we drove onto the
dam and then onto the Chernavsky bridge and across the Voronezh
River. We could tell that we were now driving on an unpaved road
and we squatted down to minimize the impact of the truck boun-
cing over the many potholes. Then a kind of fortress rose in front
of us with a sign above the heavy door that read "Voronezh Suvorov

---

2 Voronezh was the scene of fierce fighting between the German and Soviet armies
   in 1942 and 1943 and was almost totally destroyed. The Germans used the city as
   an important staging area for their attack on Stalingrad.

Military School." The superintendent of the school came out, spoke briefly to the escorting officer and then gave the order to open the gates. We were dropped off at one of the barracks where we spent the night on mattresses on the floor.

I had a silly and childish fight, or actually more like a confrontation, with some boys from Yugoslavia that very first night. It was a test of strength rather than a display of hatred and it didn't last long. Still, my first moments in the new environment of a military school among new guys were rather rough. The night went by quickly.

In the morning we were all taken to the bathhouse located in the school courtyard. When all the boys were undressing to enter the bathhouse, I hesitated, trying to think of how to hide the fact that I had been circumcised. How would the other boys react? Would they make fun of me? I was the only Jewish boy there. As it turned out, however, the bathhouse was very crowded, so no one noticed anything. Still, my heart raced until I was able to put my clothes back on. We had all been given new uniforms, which everyone liked.

After the bathhouse we went to the cafeteria. On the second floor we saw a table covered with a snow-white tablecloth and precisely set with fine china. I also noticed white biscuits. I had never seen such a table – not as a child, obviously not in the forest, not at the field hospital – not even in my dreams. At the field hospital our dinnerware had been limited to a bowl and a spoon. Here we began to acquire discipline and order and a sense of etiquette right away. We filed to the table one by one and stood facing our seats waiting for the command to sit down. Less than ten minutes later breakfast was over.

The first stage of our assimilation into military school life was the introduction of all the new recruits to the current cadets. I was assigned to an advanced group that included three other sons of the regiment: Nikolai (Kolya) Potozky, Victor Zhuk and Ivan (Vanya) Makarov. The war had interrupted our studies and now we all had to catch up, but my task was even more difficult. Since my first language was Yiddish and my Russian was mostly self-taught, aside from the few lessons I'd had with Captain Musihin's wife, my Russian-language skills were very poor.

We were assigned to the 3rd Platoon of the 6th Company. Our teacher and supervisor was Captain Zavialov. The Suvorov Military School was founded in 1943 and offered an education based on the principles of the pre-Soviet Russian cadet academies. The bedside book of all the teachers and supervisors at the school was *Fifty Years of Service* by General Alexei A. Ignatiev.[3] Our education at the school had some complicated and peculiar aspects to it because the USSR was a communist country ruled by the dictator Joseph Stalin, with his omnipresent "cult of personality."[4] The school aimed to instil faith in Stalin's Communist Party in us, but I realize now that in practice this goal was only secondary – we were primarily taught the values of group loyalty, friendship and teamwork.

The military school became our home and our family, as well as our school. Every day started with morning physical exercises, followed by classes and study hall, all confined to the school's four walls. Eventually it all became routine. As our friendships developed, various groups formed and fought for dominance. The arrival of the sons of the regiments – me among them – threatened the dominant position of the older cadets and undermined their control over the younger cadets. So the older cadets tried to separate us and make us quarrel. The older cadets also bullied the younger ones into giving up their fruits, juice and sunflower seeds. These moments were silly, but nevertheless some boys were scared. My group, which came to-

---

3 *Fifty Years of Service* is the memoir of General Alexei A. Ignatiev, a general under Tsar Nicholas II who became a Soviet general and a Hero of the Soviet Union after the Russian Revolution in 1918.

4 Stalin actively created a "cult of personality" using the media to present himself as a god-like and infallible father to the USSR. His portrait was hung in homes and public buildings, and artists and poets were legally required to produce only works that glorified him.

gether over the course of several years, included Novik Sidorov, Boris Plotnik, Kolya Potozky and some others. Our group was monolithic, tight and respected because some of us were sons of the regiments. Over the years, it only grew stronger, and I became a leader.

The teachers at the school were the best in the Voronezh region, and I worked hard studying Russian and other subjects. I will never forget the attention I received from my teachers. A. S. Milovidov taught Russian language and literature; A. I. Darmodehina, mathematics; M. N. Postnikov, physics; S. N. Kolesnev, chemistry; P. M. Markina, geography; A. M. Kikot, French; S. V. Finin and Tutukov, physical culture (our term for gym class), and many others. I could write a lot about each one of them. They were mostly officers from the front lines of the recently ended war who had prior military and educational training. They took their task seriously, as if a great responsibility weighed heavily on their shoulders. Working now on special methods of educating and raising war orphans and children who had been brought up by single mothers in poverty and famine, they sought to turn us into the elite officers of the future. They regarded us as raw material and tried to mould us into individuals faithful to the Soviet people and the Communist Party, although, as I said, not many of us paid much attention to Party loyalty then. We mainly got a good education, excellent physical conditioning and, most importantly, developed faithful ties of friendship that withstood the test of many years. The school took its mandate to prepare competent future military personnel seriously and made every effort to recruit the best teachers and counsellors. I profoundly thank my teachers from the bottom of my heart. Many of them are no longer with us, but they have stayed in my heart.

I think my early experiences and fear of death at the hands of the Nazis taught me survival skills that the other boys didn't have. I had to put extra effort into my studies, for example, but I had to find a way to do so without the other boys noticing. No one liked extra-diligent students – they were scornfully called *zubrila*. Every night I used to hide in a bathroom stall and stay up to all hours memorizing my homework for the next day.

As time went on, I became more and more confident that I could handle all the lessons given to us by the teachers. Apart from our regular lessons in traditional subjects, we also underwent tough military training and studied aesthetics, ethics, logic, psychology and, in an interesting twist, ballroom dancing. We were encouraged to be open-minded and seek beauty in every person and every living thing. The sound of students reciting the great poet Pushkin's words, "My friends, our union is delightful…"[5] echoed through the halls.

Despite my belonging to a strong group of boys who protected each other, I did experience an antisemitic outburst from one of the older cadets. I had been assigned to dig a hole by the volleyball court and a boy passing by remarked, "Hey, Jew, are you digging a grave for yourself?" I lost control and hit him over the head with my shovel without considering the possible consequences. Since no one from my group was there to help me and this boy was much stronger than me, I got hurt myself. This incident made me more careful.

I became the best student academically and actively participated in all school activities. There were many opportunities to get involved. Who would've thought that after this brutal war we would start learning ballroom dancing? That we'd jump around in mazurka, float in pas zefir and pas d'espagne, and Boston waltz, foxtrot and soft tango? It was an extreme change for me as a Jewish boy brought up in a strict Jewish household with kosher food, prayers in the synagogue and an elementary education in Yiddish-speaking cheder, but resourcefulness, common sense and wit motivated and guided me.

Studying in close quarters in an all-male school, we were naturally interested in girls. They excited our imagination and our fantasies ran wild. We had a lot of energy! So in my second or third year at the

---

5   From Alexander Pushkin's poem "October 19th," published in 1825.

school, we got the idea of arranging a series of meetings with girls from the all-girls' schools in the region, starting with school No. 23 in Pridacha. We formed a theatre club and picked a play that had four female parts and approached the administration of the military school for permission to invite some of the girls from school No. 23 to join the cast. They agreed.

Along with the rehearsals, we managed to find some time to be alone with these girls, to dance and even to have little romances. These were innocent childish crushes, but in some cases they grew into first love. Valentina (Valya) Grinkevich was the first girl I got to know from the theatre club. She was a fragile girl with a little nose, who lived with her parents in a small house. Her house was not far from the military school, so I cherished the hope that we could continue our relationship during my infrequent and brief leaves.

Our meetings gradually grew in frequency, both on and off stage. She was mesmerized by my stories of life in the military school and on the front lines. Neither of us had had any previous experience in love relationships, but the body calls for unknown pleasures and, not thinking of the consequences, we pursued our passions. It happened at her house in the summertime when her parents were away. I came over wearing my summer uniform, which consisted of a white shirt and black pants with red vertical stripes. The sparks flew and everything happened very quickly. However, our fear that her parents would arrive unexpectedly prevented us from enjoying the pleasure we had read about in books. Later meetings gave us the opportunity to indulge a little more.

The days flew by at school and I had little free time. Along with a heavy academic load, I also actively competed in sports. The gym hall was enormous and we spent a lot of time there in training sessions and in various competitions between teams from different classes, companies and towns. I participated in school cup competitions in basketball, soccer, fencing and community cross-country running events. My results were rather good. I ran the 100-metre race in 11.6

seconds and was one of the school's top ten fencers. This athletic success was the result of rigorous training inspired by my desire to earn the respect of my peers and the administration.

As I've said, life at the military school was filled with lessons and sport practices, so we had little time to ourselves. We spent most of our hours and days inside the four walls of the school and it was difficult to escape, to breathe free air and to meet local boys and girls. The privilege of weekend leave had to be earned by hard work, exemplary behaviour and flawless appearance. I recall endless inspections to determine who was eligible for weekend release. The boys who were denied leave had to rely on other boys' stories of the fun they had had for excitement.

Methods of discipline were refined as the years progressed, but discipline was generally built on the principle of "all for one and one for all." A typical collective punishment when someone committed some infraction was an exhausting company march all the way to Otrozhki, a few kilometres from Voronezh. The actual culprits were also put into the school's punishment cell left over from the time the building had been a state prison. It was a narrow room with a cement floor and a tiny opening in the ceiling to allow in sparse sunlight. I saw this cell but was lucky enough never to have to spend time there.

Many boys spent their energy on various naughty escapades. I too participated in the so-called raids on the bread trucks and some attacks on the kitchen. That's how we used to get extra bread and meat cutlets. We didn't do it because we were hungry but to test each boy's loyalty to the group. It was nothing more than childish mischief, a way to release some energy. We also sometimes got into mischief with some teachers. Our French teacher was an old lady from tsarist times who tried to teach us the language and acquaint us with French culture and literature. But the boys were downright cruel to her. I also recall an incident with the geography teacher. The boys found out about her intimate relationship with a local major and constantly giggled and made remarks.

Across from our school were barracks housing German POWs, a constant reminder of the recent war. We could see them from our second-floor windows playing soccer or getting into trucks to work on the reconstruction of Voronezh, which the Germans had badly damaged. Sometimes, when we got a weekend release, we jumped onto those trucks to get into the city faster. I remember asking the Germans where they had fought. They replied that most of them had been in supply-line companies. As children of the war, it was interesting to see a different side of these infamous fighting cocks.

The so-called Suvorov summer consisted of a one-month vacation, during which everyone went home, and two months spent at a summer camp. We lived in tents out in nature, in the fields, and hiked to various historic places in the vicinity of Voronezh such as Semiluki, Ramon, Usman and others. One of our summer campsites was near the famous Ramon settlement gardens on the west bank of the Voronezh River. Our camp was situated on the edge of the magnificent gardens, but we were forbidden to pick any fruit for fear of a dysentery outbreak. A stone line separating the camp from the gardens was painted white and we called it the "general line."

I also remember an incident that happened at the Semiluki summer camp between the Don and Deviza rivers. We developed a plan to secretly raid some nearby watermelon fields. During the quietest hour of the afternoon a group of boys and I secretly crossed the Deviza river on a small boat and headed toward the fields, but the mission was only partly successful because a guard noticed us and started shouting and firing his gun into the air. We carried watermelons however we could – in our shirts and in our interlocked hands – as we ran for the boat. Then, once we had loaded the watermelons, we couldn't find the paddles. We had to paddle by hand all the way to the other side. That was the end of our raid. The watermelons were sweet, though….

Sometimes we would sabotage study hall. That was easy. We'd use a needle to short-circuit the electrical lines in the building and put the power out so we wouldn't be asked for our homework the next day. Soon our childish naughtiness turned into teenage bravado. One example was taking unauthorized leave, which usually resulted in heavy reprimands. I think that our escapades were both positive and negative – in some ways we were showing what we saw as courage and heroism, and in others we were just showing off. But nevertheless we grew older and more mature, and the school staff successfully prepared us as highly qualified army men.

My persistence in studies and school activities had earned me a high ranking in my class. In fact, I had advanced fairly rapidly in my studies, although I was at first behind the students in my age group. I quickly caught up and after studying hard over my first summer at the cadet school I advanced into the appropriate education level for my age. In my new grade there were ten sons of the regiment. By 1951, I was nineteen years old and it was almost time for final exams and preparing for graduation.

Just as not all cadets of the tsarist times ended up as officers but became writers, inventors, and the like, not all the Suvorov cadets stayed in the military. Indeed, my destiny was to be different – rough and sometimes unfair.

Prior to graduation I, along with another Suvorov cadet, was offered an opportunity to join the Communist Party of the Soviet Union.[6] It was, however, 1951, in the middle of Stalin's infamous antisemitic campaign. Although I went through all the training and the paperwork, I was denied membership in the end. Party officials had received information from someone in Rokitno stating that my father had been a Jewish propagandist who dealt in Jewish literature. That wasn't true and I still don't know who provided that false information.

---

6 Becoming a member of the Communist Party was vitally important for furthering one's career in the Soviet Union as it confirmed one's allegiance to the nation and to the principles of the U S S R. Regardless of whether one was, in fact, a devout communist, joining the Party was a crucial step in professional advancement.

Looking back I understand that this was part of yet another period of heavy persecution and harassment of Jews in the Soviet Union. In 1948 Stalin had launched an open campaign to rid the Communist Party, the government, and even literature, of Jews.[7] At that time, I was shocked when I read news reports accusing that great man, Solomon Mikhoels, the head of the Jewish Anti-Fascist Committee, of being a "bourgeois Jewish nationalist" and a "double secret agent" of the United States and the Joint – the American Jewish Joint Distribution Committee, a Jewish aid agency.[8] The newspapers reported that Mikhoels had been killed by bandits in Minsk, although he was actually murdered by the authorities. By the end of 1948 the Jewish Anti-Fascist Committee had been closed down along with the Yiddish newspaper *Eynikayt* and the last of the Jewish schools. Jewish cultural leaders and writers, including ardent communists like Itzik Feffer, were arrested and later executed.

These antisemitic policies escalated in the early 1950s and culminated in 1953, the year of Stalin's death. In 1951 and 1952 there was a general purge of Jews from the sciences, the field of technology, the professions, academia, the arts and the military. On January 13, 1953, the Soviet news agency TASS announced the infamous "Doctors' Plot." A group of doctors, most of them Jewish, were accused of espionage and plotting the murder of leading government and party

---

7 Between 1948 and 1953, Stalin embarked on a targeted campaign against Soviet Jews as part of a broad and extreme anti-Western cultural policy campaign known as the Zhdanovshchina (after Andrei Zhdanov, the Party Central Committee secretary for ideology). Stalin accused Jews of lacking full allegiance to the Soviet Union and many were arrested on false charges, tried and sentenced to hard labour or execution. For more information, see both the glossary and the introduction.

8 The American Jewish Joint Distribution Committee – more popularly known as the "Joint" or JDC – was established during World War I and charged with distributing funds raised by the American Jewish charities for the relief of Jews in Europe and Palestine. It continues to assist Jews worldwide to this day.

officials. The press called them "saboteur-doctors," but all were in fact innocent.

All this was the backdrop for my graduation day at the Suvorov school. On that fateful day in June 1951, everyone but me lined up to take his military oath. I wasn't allowed. Despite the fact that I graduated from the Suvorov school with a silver medal – supposedly guaranteeing me a place at whatever military officer school I chose – I wasn't allowed to even take the oath. It was a terrible shock to me, and to all of my closest friends as well. They tried to cheer me up with encouraging words, but they were helpless to change anything. I paced in the courtyard, trapped by its four walls. I didn't know what destiny had in store for me now. What would I do as a civilian? Continue to study at an institute? I didn't have any money for tuition. I felt that my world was empty again.

After graduation, the military school grew quiet as all the boys left for summer vacation or to their newly assigned placements for further study or military service. But I had been left behind at the school and the administration didn't know what to do with me. They were probably waiting for orders from higher echelons. It was as if I had become an orphan again. Dark thoughts clouded my head, but my survival instincts prevailed. Finally, the powers that be decided what to do with me and I was allowed to take my oath on September 26, 1951. I was assigned to continue my studies and do my service at the Kiev infantry military school – a much less prestigious posting than the one I would have chosen.

I left the Voronezh Suvorov Military School with mixed feelings. On one hand, I was grateful to my teachers, to my friends who believed in me and to the home the school had provided me. On the other hand, I felt a heavy sense of injustice. I understand now that my frustration should have been aimed at all dictatorial systems run by maniacs and supported by local greedy spongers. First Hitler and now Stalin. This was the second time in my life that I witnessed a coordinated effort to persecute my people.

My Military Career

In September 1951, at nineteen years of age, I reluctantly but with fond memories said goodbye to the Suvorov home where I had come of age. I was embittered about leaving for Kiev since I had been assigned to an infantry military school of much lower status than the more prestigious future I had worked so hard to earn. My new school was located on a small cobblestone street named Kerosennaya and its barracks were on a hill. Once again I found my freedom restricted and defined by fences and checkpoints and other such impediments. I was assigned to a company consisting of Suvorov Military School alumni from different Suvorov schools around the country. Major Chuchmansky, commander of this company, was of middle height with a serious face. Since we were all former Suvorov cadets, all of the boys got acquainted quickly. Three of my fellow Voronezh alumni were here in Kiev as well: Valerian Golyageen, Evgenyi (Zhenya) Chistyakov and Igor Ryabkov.

The course of study here was fairly short, only two years. But those were the two years – 1951 to 1953 – when the wave of antisemitism in the Soviet Union reached its peak. There were incidents in Podol (an old district of Kiev) in which Jews were thrown off trams and sometimes were beaten. The newspapers were filled with slanders about Jewish doctors because of the so-called Doctor's Plot. It was in this atmosphere that I tried to better myself as a soldier and prepare myself to be an officer. Perhaps significantly, I didn't feel any hostility or distrust from my classmates. For them I was only their fellow Suvorov cadet. I was a diligent student who kept up with the others in class, during military training and in marching drills.

Every weekend we got leave to go into town. Our desire to leave campus and mingle with local residents was very strong. Our regular hangout was the basement of Fred Zolotkovsky's parents' house, which was near the historic Golden Gate of Kiev.[1] Fred's father, Munus Semyonovich, and his mother, Sofa, also had two daughters, Marina and Zhanna, who lived there. Munus was a retired major, a World War II veteran whose personality was characterized by wisdom, humour and zest for life. He was our friend and advisor. Sofa was a dutiful wife with a warm motherly Jewish heart. She always made sure that we had enough to eat. Their home was a haven of freedom for all of the Suvorov boys who came by.

This chapter in my life was unremarkable – full of typical military drills and minutiae. For us Suvorov graduates the classes were very easy, even rudimentary. Our group mastered the basics of military training faster than all the others. Our training in Kiev paid special attention not only to physical exercise, but also to the study of tactics and the newest weaponry. The Kalashnikov AK-47 machine gun had just been developed and before we could put our hands on it we were required to swear that we would keep our knowledge top secret. During shooting practice we were held accountable for every bullet and every cartridge. Sometimes after practice we had to go out in the field with torches and melt the snow and ice to find the missing bullets.

My time at the infantry school in Kiev went by quickly and once

---

1   The Golden Gate of Kiev was one of three gates to the city constructed in the mid-eleventh century. Reputedly named for and modelled on the Golden Gate of Constantinople, the original gate fell into ruins but was excavated and reconstructed in the nineteenth century.

again we found ourselves getting ready for graduation and now, induction into our first military rank – lieutenant. As the day approached, our group of Suvorov graduates decided to organize a reunion of Suvorov alumni in Voronezh. We made a map of all the places where our classmates had gone to continue their education and then made plans for the event and distributed flyers calling for a reunion in Voronezh, timed to coincide with the next Suvorov Military School graduation in September 1953.

I was reassigned to a Kiev military district division and stationed in the town of Lubny in the Poltava region.[2] Before relocating there, however, we got an extended leave of absence for the trip to Voronezh. Valerian (Valera) Golyageen and I set up a meeting with a few Suvorov alumni, including Igor Ryabkov, in Petrovsky Park in Voronezh to discuss the details of our reunion. Many young officers came. Most of them managed to come because they had just received their first paycheques. It was a very interesting reunion because we were joined not only by members of our class but also by older alumni who were now experienced officers.

When the school administration found out about this massive student-organized reunion, they called me and Valera in. They chastised us for not informing them in advance and for not reporting directly to the school (our former home), staying instead in hotels and people's houses. All the alumni attending the reunion were ordered to report immediately to the military school. Beds with snow-white sheets were placed in the gym where young cadets stood on honour guard.

This reunion showed that the tradition of friendship had grown into a tradition of brotherhood and these reunions became an annual event. We were maturing, gaining more military as well as civilian experience. Friendship and memories of our kind teachers filled our

2 Lubny is an ancient Ukrainian town, located approximately 180 kilometres from Kiev.

souls, the souls of the children of war. It was a very emotional reunion for us as well as for current cadets, teachers and, of course, our former girlfriends, who were very eager to see us again. We all shared stories, memories and opinions about various things.

We also listened to the stories of those who had helped to train and equip troops in Egypt and Syria.[3] I was greatly interested in that because by this time I had learned from Aunt Roza that my brothers, Natan and Samuel, were living in Israel. I must say that I heard objective evaluations of the competency and capabilities of the Arab militaries, and I heard many stories about Israeli army training as well. I was very anxious to learn more about that part of the world.

As planned, the reunion coincided with the 1953 Suvorov Military School graduation. The tables were set in the cafeteria in the shape of the Russian letter for P, that is, it looked like this: П. The administration sat on one side with graduating cadets on the other, while alumni and teachers shared the third side. I sat next to our chemistry teacher and three of my closest friends, Novik, Valera and Boris.

Arsik Kolumbov was the first to propose a toast. Since alcohol consumption was officially banned at the military school, Kolumbov raised the toast with a non-alcoholic beverage. Our former chemistry teacher, however, argued that, historically speaking, army officers never celebrated anything without a stiff drink. Consequently the waitresses were quietly ordered to bring in bottles of liquor on the condition that no alcohol would be served to the young cadets.

After the banquet there was a concert and a dance, but that didn't end the celebration. The next day it continued at a restaurant. We in-

---

3   In the mid-1950s, the USSR signed agreements with both Egypt and Syria for military and economic cooperation. These included the provision of military advisors, arms and economic assistance in return for which Egypt and Syria refused to support British and American policies in the Middle East, particularly the Baghdad Pact that formally allied several other states in the region with the United States and Britain.

vited our teachers and mentors, but not the administrators. The gathering turned into a real drunken riot and I was actually arrested by the Voronezh commandant's police as "an organizer of group binge drinking." Bearing this latest label I went on to Lubny to join my new regiment, where the highly organized life quickly drew me back into military discipline. I was made commander of a company and was soon reassigned to a sniper training camp. I must confess that the days went by in devastating boredom and every night the senior officers drank bootleg vodka that they bought in nearby villages.

Life in Lubny was dull and gray. The young officers went to dances at the officers' club and sometimes to private parties held by girls in their homes. My goal was to continue my education and get a degree in engineering and I used every opportunity I could find to apply to a military academy. Getting another qualification was the only way that it might be possible for me to make up what I had lost when I was denied a more prestigious commission after graduating from the Suvorov school. My first attempt was to apply to the academy of communications in Leningrad. I wrote the entry examinations in Kiev, and Igor Ryabkov and I successfully passed, but once again I was summarily denied admission to the academy.

I can assure you now that only one thing prejudiced the administration and prevented me from being admitted: the fifth paragraph in my Soviet passport that identified me as Jewish.[4] Despite this setback, I managed to keep in good spirits and continued my service.

Shortly after this, in the fall of 1954, I was reassigned to the 51st Motorized Infantry Regiment in the town of Kandalaksha in the

---

4 In the Soviet Union, every person over the age of sixteen had to carry an internal "passport." In addition to personal information such as name and date of birth, every internal Soviet passport issued after 1936 also included the so-called "fifth paragraph" stating the bearer's "nationality," which, as defined in the USSR, might be Russian, Ukrainian, Kazakh, Estonian, etc. – or Jew (in Russian, *Yivrei*). The information in this fifth paragraph was often used to discriminate against Soviet Jews.

northern polar military district,[5] where Colonel Kobetz was the commander. My military life continued there without any changes except for the very different climate. Summer that far north is the season of "white nights," as we called it, when it's always light outside and for six months you can't tell the difference between day and night. The only indication that it's evening is that the bright sun moves lower in the sky, closer to the horizon line. Then polar night comes and the darkness lasts for another six months.

This part of the country was famous for its close proximity to the North Pole – and in Russian we call it Zapolarie, which simply means "near the pole." Historically, many prisons had been located in the town and prison inmates, including many women, built the large Niva-3 electric power station on the Niva River that ends in Kandalashka. The inmates lived in barracks and in stationary train cars all lined up one next to another with a bright light pole next to each building.

Another peculiarity of the place was the large quantity of salmon you could get, usually caught in the canals during spawning. Even though this military town was fairly isolated it had its cultural centre – the officer's club where various activities were conducted. Interestingly, there was a rather large contingent of Jews here in this harsh and bleak part of the globe. Among the officers were doctors, musicians, minesweepers and others. I spent more than three years in service in this tundra of low greenish swamps and small stone hills. In these harsh conditions I learned a lot about the positive and negative sides of life, but I must confess that I had more negative than positive feelings at the time.

Even in this gray and cold part of the country, however, there was one very bright ray of hope. I met my future wife in these bleak con-

---

5 Kandalaksha is located at the head of Kandalaksha Gulf on the White Sea, seventy-two kilometres north of the Arctic circle. It is approximately 885 kilometres north of Leningrad (now called Saint Petersburg).

ditions. I was at a party hosted by our mutual friends the Polotzkiy and Katz families. They introduced me to Marina Zeitlina, who had come to Kandalaksha as a doctor right after her graduation from the Moscow Medical Institute. Our meetings at the homes of Tamara and Alik Polotzkiy or Rimma and Gregory (Grisha) Katz became more and more frequent. During these meetings we told each other the stories of our lives and our families. We talked about our education and, of course, we often discussed the issue of antisemitism. Our experiences had been very different, but our friendship grew stronger every day. This was my only solace in the far north.

Tamara Polotzkaya was also a doctor at a Kandalaksha hospital and her husband, Alik, was an officer in a special communications battalion. We often talked about Tamara's parents. Her father, Mark Yakovlevich Tzipin, was a war veteran and a military doctor. After the war he was one of the people accused in the Doctors' Plot. He was convicted but later pardoned. The Polotzkiy family was wonderful and we enjoyed knowing them.

Rimma Katz was another doctor and her husband, Grisha, was a minesweeper. Grisha and I served in the same division and participated in many military training sessions and drills together. For almost two years, during the summers, we performed the critical task of clearing the minefields along the border with Finland.[6] Clearing the minefields was very tedious and mundane – and also dangerous. While our regiment was performing this risky work we were stationed in the same areas that had been occupied by German forces during World War II and our battalion was housed in the same barracks that had been formerly used by Nazi soldiers.

I once again witnessed the death and wounding of soldiers and officers. I was lucky because there were no casualties in my regiment.

---

6 When the Germans retreated from occupied Finland at the end of World War II, they left behind almost a quarter of a million landmines along the Soviet-Finnish border.

I was ordered to escort the bodies of dead soldiers to the cemetery in the Zapolarie region. To do that, we often had to take boats across many of the local lakes. What a bitter paradox! Here we were escorting a casket by boat, surrounded by breathtaking landscapes and intoxicating natural beauty. We sailed by tiny, perfectly round islands with birch groves. Fish jumped out of the water and glistened in the light of the bright, cold sun. In such beauty and silence, it's impossible to believe in death even in its presence.

In the summer there were legions of mosquitoes that came in clouds of tiny bugs during the day, and that played an annoying symphony of buzzing at night. These insects constantly drew blood from our legs. In these harsh conditions we were subjected to new training standards set forth by an order of the minister of defense, Marshal Zhukov. I especially remember winter drills in which I had to sleep in cave-like holes that the soldiers dug in the snow. It was so cold that sometimes we'd even build a fire inside the holes and the walls wouldn't melt. Anyone who has ever served in the army knows what tactical drills are – now imagine them done beyond the polar circle in winter! This was a test of will and character, meant to prepare us for the most difficult of missions.

I got such a test immediately after I arrived in Kandalaksha – a two-day, forty-eight-hour cross-country skiing marathon through the frost. We only took our skis off during short breaks en route and to sleep in the deep snow banks of Zapolarie. Our group of skiers, in white camouflage gear, moved very slowly. I was the leader of my regiment and had to be the first to make the tracks. However, it was so difficult that we all had to rotate positions every two hundred metres. During this long trek, we also endured entrenchment, mock attacks and simulated contamination. As soon as they heard the order to stop for a break, most of the soldiers passed out from exhaustion. We had to conduct continual roster calls to make sure that no one froze to death in their sleep. The field training, which seemed interminable, finally came to an end and we were ordered to return to base. Everyone was deeply exhausted and couldn't wait to get back home.

Our only opportunities to have fun were restricted to visits with understanding friends and various evening programs at the officers' club. That's where I met the conductor of the district orchestra, Major Mikhail Aronovich Safian, a short and stout but very energetic man. When people first met Mikhail, they were usually taken aback by his slight speech impediment and the nervous twitching of his mouth. But he had a great influence on me. He was full of energy, especially when conducting. He was a Jewish war veteran, a famous wartime composer and conductor, author of a popular poem, "Odessa, Hero City," and a mentor to a whole group of distinguished musicians. He was a true "Odessit" – a native of Odessa, the Ukrainian port city on the Black Sea. He was proud of his city, its humour, its people, the beauty of its streets and its clear sea air.

Shortly before I left the country I met Safian again in Odessa and he vowed he would never leave his city. But history proved that even for this extremely talented man there was no future in Russia for Jews. Many years later I came across a newspaper article about his seventy-fifth birthday and decided to seek him out. This time, it was under very different circumstances. I found him, unexpectedly, in the famous Brighton Beach neighbourhood of New York, coincidentally also a port city.[7]

Meanwhile, the gray routine of the cold north made my determination to continue my education even stronger. I applied again to study engineering, this time to the automobile transport department of the Military Academy of the Civilian Home Front and Transportation in Leningrad (now St. Petersburg). I was rejected on the basis of the same entry in my passport. Losing hope, I went on with my service.

---

7 Brighton Beach is a community in Brooklyn, New York, that has been called "Little Odessa" because so many of its residents are immigrants from that city.

The Khruschev Era

It took significant political upheaval before anything changed in my own situation. Nothing developed until Stalin died in March 1953. When Nikita Sergeevich Khrushchev came into power, he instituted what became known as the "thaw."[1] Almost immediately after Stalin's death, the atmosphere in the country began to change – for example, the charges against the Jewish doctors were dropped and the planned purge was called off. Especially after 1956, when Khrushchev denounced what he called the "crimes of the Stalin-era," the Stalin cult of personality began to fade.[2] The publication of Solzhenitsyn's *One Day in the Life of Ivan Denisovich,* a story of life in the gulag labour camps, was a clear indication that things had changed.[3]

---

1 Nikita Khrushchev served as first Secretary of the Communist Party of the Soviet Union from 1953 to 1964. For more information, see the glossary.

2 In 1956, Khrushchev made a special report to 20th Party Congress in Moscow in which he denounced Stalin's dictatorship and cult of personality but maintained the ideals of Communism. The so-called "secret speech," which was soon reported to the press, led to a period of liberalization in the USSR. The repression that had become so commonplace was overturned to some extent and millions of political prisoners were released.

3 *One Day in the Life of Ivan Denisovich,* a novel written by Alexander Solzhenitsyn, was first published in November 1962 in the Soviet literary magazine *Novy Mir* (New World). Set in a Soviet labour camp in the 1950s, the novel describes a single day of an ordinary prisoner who is accused of being a spy after he returns

In the midst of these changes, I decided to try my luck and applied to continue my education for the third time. I applied to the military communication department of that same Military Academy of the Civilian Home Front and Transportation in Leningrad. This time my application was accepted, but as the academy was going to admit only five people into the program, I would have to pass the entrance exams. Since I had graduated from the Suvorov school with a silver medal, however, I was only required to take one mandatory exam in mathematics.

When I arrived in Leningrad to take the exam, I ran into Zhiharevich, the former commissar of the field hospital. It turned out that after demobilization she had come to Leningrad and been appointed an academic dean of the distance education department of the Leningrad Institute of Cinema Engineering. Our reunion was very heartfelt. She introduced me to her brother, who was a math teacher. He gave me some quizzes and after reviewing my answers decided that I was ready to take any math exam. During subsequent meetings with this wonderful educated man I learned more about his past. He had fought on the front lines until he was captured by the Germans. He survived and returned to his hometown of Leningrad, where he was arrested and sent to prison as a "traitor."[4] He was later

---

from being a prisoner of war in Germany and is sent to Siberia. The open distribution of this outspoken account of Stalinist repression was an extraordinary and unprecedented event in Soviet literary history.

4 Many Soviet POWs returned home after the war only to be arrested, imprisoned, sent to hard labour or executed. By the "Catch-22" logic of Stalin's USSR, they were considered traitors because "if they had fought hard enough," they certainly wouldn't have been captured, and having been captured they must only have survived because they had "collaborated." The real reason for this policy was a paranoid fear that any Soviet citizen who had lived in a Western European country – even as a prisoner – could have been corrupted by their exposure to the capitalist West and might, on their return to the USSR, spread their capitalist ways or agitate for reform. Many of these prisoners were pardoned and freed after Khrushchev came to power and denounced Stalin.

declared "wrongly accused" and was pardoned. There were many documented cases like his.

I passed the entrance exams and was enrolled in the academy in 1957. With Stalin gone, I would now finally be able to advance my education and my career – or so I thought. Before I said goodbye to my friends in Zapolarie, I had decided that I wanted to spend my life with one particular person who had shared my long northern days, namely Marina Zeitlina. She was planning a vacation in the south, so I suggested that she come by and visit me in Leningrad on her way. She met me there and after some discussion, we decided to part maintaining the status quo. She went south and I stayed in Leningrad.

Preparation for the new school year began. I was assigned a dorm room and then, after a meeting with the chairman of the department of fuels and lubricants, I agreed to transfer to that department. Studying at the academy was not easy, but I was living my dream. I felt that I would only survive in this country where antisemitism was open and common by being successful in my studies. The course of study that I was in would take five years and led to a diploma in military mechanical engineering – the equivalent of a North American engineering degree. During this time I met and formed relationships with many other students. Most of them were married and already had stable families. I was still a bachelor.

I spent my years at the academy – from 1957 to 1962 – not only studying but also exploring the wonderful Hero City of Leningrad.[5] The signs and scars of the cruel war were noticeable everywhere. I met a few of the city natives who had survived the terrible siege of Leningrad. Every now and then I saw some of them in the cafeteria of the Mariinsky Theater where I often stopped to grab a bite.

---

5 The honorary designation of "Hero City" was awarded to twelve cities in the Soviet Union for the outstanding heroism of their citizens during World War II. Leningrad had survived 872 days of siege by the Nazis and sustained one million casualties.

My dormitory was located nearby at No. 2 Glinka Street. Living in the heart of the city, I often went to the museums and theatres and on weekends I went dancing. Despite the availability of a multitude of cultural events – in stark contrast to my previous place of residence – I was lonely and wanted to settle down. I soon received a letter from Marina. She was planning to visit me in Leningrad on her way back to Kandalaksha from the Black Sea resort of Hosta in the south. It wasn't long before I was walking with Marina along Nevsky Prospect, the main and grand boulevard of the city. It was a clear day. The sun was shining brightly, its rays illuminating the great monument on the Anichkov Bridge.[6] As we strolled along we came to the popular Nord café and I suggested that we go in for a cup of coffee. I asked Marina to be my wife. She accepted!

We quickly began planning the official ceremony. Since we were not far away from the civil registry office, we decided to file all the necessary paperwork and get married right away, but we were told that we would have to wait a month. We didn't consider this acceptable, so I decided to see if there was any way that we could get around the restriction. I brought a box of chocolates to the girls who worked in the registry office and proceeded to plead with them to expedite the process before Marina had to return to work up north. My efforts were successful and we were married three days later, on September 30, 1957.

We celebrated our marriage by buying a bottle of champagne and going to where Marina was staying with her relatives. They were very excited and even managed to come up with a spontaneous dinner reception. That was our first wedding celebration. The next day my lawful wife left for Kandalaksha to say goodbye to that gray northern land before returning to Leningrad and our future. Despite the sim-

---

6 The Anichkov bridge is known for the four impressive nineteenth-century bronze corner statues – *The Horse Tamers* – designed by the Russian sculptor, Baron Peter Klodt von Urgensburg.

plicity and confusion of the whole affair, I must say that our wedding was quite romantic.

My search for housing now began. I started going to the Malkov bazaar where people advertised rooms and sometimes whole apartments for rent. It reminded me of the famous Privoz food market, the largest in Odessa. All my efforts to get a room through the academy proved futile because the upperclassmen had priority in housing. Apartment hunting in this city was a very long process, but I wasn't in a terrible rush. We had decided that after coming back south, Marina and I would go to Moscow together so we could have a wedding with her family that we now planned for the following February.

My vacation was coming up. I was very excited and looked forward to it with much anticipation. In Moscow I met Marina's parents for the second time – the first had been on a summer vacation in 1956 – but I didn't get to meet the rest of her family. Her father, Aaron Grigorievich Zeitlin, was a man with a strong build and a wide forehead that looked even wider because he was balding. He was very smart, very tactful, and also a great handyman – a man with what we call "golden hands." He was chemist by profession, a graduate of the Mendeleev Institute. His childhood had begun in the small village of Seno in the Vitebsk region of Belarus, halfway between Minsk and Smolensk. His family was large and to make sure that there was enough food for everyone, he started working at age fourteen as an assistant to a pharmacist. He was brought up in a strict Orthodox Jewish family similar to my own. While he worked in the pharmacy he continued to be true to his Jewish roots. His native tongue was Yiddish. He and his brothers eventually moved to Moscow where he married Rita Moiseevna Zeitlin – they had the same last name even though they weren't related at all.

Marina's mother, Rita Moiseevna, also came from a poor Jewish family, in Melitopol, a small city in the southern part of Ukraine. After she graduated from a lyceum (high school), she came to Moscow, studied at the medical institute and became a doctor. At the beginning of World War II, Aaron Grigorievich was drafted to serve in the military. His family was evacuated from Moscow in July 1941 to the town of Khvalynsk on the Volga River in the Saratov Region. The evacuation was hard on Marina's family. In her own way, Marina too has suffered the horrors and the consequences of that awful war. Her family didn't starve to death – as did many who remained in Moscow – but Rita Moiseevna had to raise two children alone while working full-time as a doctor, caring for many sick children and trying to save them.

Our second wedding took place at the Zeitlin home on Bolshaya Filevskaya Street. It was quite an undertaking, typical of the times in the Soviet Union. Because there were severe shortages of food and other goods, everything had to be "found" so we improvised and made the arrangements through unofficial channels using personal contacts.[7] Some of my mother-in-law's patients who worked in the food industry helped us get food for the modest banquet. As for the alcoholic beverages, that was a task for my father-in-law, the famous chemist. He brewed his own liquor using his own secret recipes.

About forty people came to this wedding, mostly Marina's relatives, but also my best friend, Novik, and his remarkable mother, Tamara Akimovna. It's hard to imagine now how exactly we all fit into that tiny apartment. Thank God the people Marina's parents shared the apartment with allowed us to use their part of the flat.[8]

---

7 Like most Soviet citizens, Alex and his family had to deal with the inherent shortages and bureaucratic complexities and constraints of the Soviet economic system. This often meant risking participation in the illegal organized black market for ordinary goods and services, or informally bartering or trading for them. As a matter of everyday survival, most Soviet citizens knew how to steer through a complicated and often corrupt bureaucracy or how to, as Alex Levin tells us, "find" the consumer goods they needed.

8 Marina's family lived in a communal apartment, sharing the common spaces with another family. Such living arrangements were very common during the Soviet era, especially in large cities.

They were even nice enough to give up their bedroom for our first night as husband and wife. That was as romantic as things could get in those days.

After this vacation we returned to Leningrad together and began actively looking for an apartment and employment for Marina. Thanks to a reference from some of our friends in Kandalaksha we were given a basement room in an officers' house on the school grounds of the Leningrad Higher First Artillery Command School. We had to go through a checkpoint every time we returned home.

Our living conditions were indescribable and reminded me of the basement in Gorky's play *The Lower Depths*. Of course, I'd seen far worse conditions as a child, but my wife had a hard time adjusting to them. After a major effort, my wife found a job as a pediatrician in the 19th Outpatient Clinic of the Kirovsky borough. I continued to advance in my military and engineering studies.

And so our family life together began in Leningrad. My studies and Marina's work took up most of our time, but in our free time we went to the theatre, to movies and to museums. That was food for our souls. Academic life went on without difficulties. My classmates didn't particularly interest me. They were predominantly officers from different parts of the country who had little knowledge of mathematics and general culture. As a result of my excellent education at the Suvorov Military School I was able to tutor many of my classmates in various subjects. The semesters went by quickly. In between, we took vacations in the southern resort town of Evpatoria by the Black Sea with our friends from the north, Rimma and Grisha Katz. These were among the most pleasant days of our life together.

Over the years, however, I was haunted by memories of the ghetto and the forest. I craved an opportunity to reunite with my brothers Samuel and Natan; separation from them was like death to me. I also longed to see my only aunt who lived in Birobidzhan. My dream finally came true in 1960 when, with great difficulty, Aunt Roza came to Leningrad. This was our second meeting. The first one had taken place in Moscow, but Tamara Akimovna had kept a constant eye on us, trying to limit our communication under the guise of looking out for my best interests. In fact, Tamara Akimovna considered herself to be my surrogate mother and felt quite proprietary about me, even in relation to my own aunt, my mother's sister. No one, however, monitored or supervised this second meeting, so I was able to learn more from my aunt about my family history and about her own hard life.

I learned that my brothers, Samuel and Natan, were both still alive and had emigrated to Israel right after the war. Aunt Roza knew all this because she had been able to maintain a sporadic correspondence over the years with family members in South America who were also in touch with relatives in Israel. I also heard for the first time about the Stalin regime's cruelties toward the Jews and other ethnic minorities, and she also told me about the infamous Gulag Archipelago.[9] Roza's husband, a radio announcer, had been arrested and under extreme torture had falsely confessed to being a spy. He had been accused of blowing up a factory. He was sentenced to one of the gulags and came home such a broken man that he died shortly after his release.

Soon after my aunt's visit, Marina and I experienced a very happy event. Our daughter, Lena, was born on June 7, 1961. It was a joyous day, although I was unable to be by Marina's side during the birth. I was busy with my exams and Marina went by herself to Moscow to deliver our baby there. My life became fuller that day and I felt a great sense of responsibility for my growing family.

After studying engineering and military sciences along with Party-approved political subjects for five years, I graduated from the

---

9   The term "Gulag Archipelago" is used to describe the network of forced labour camps established by Stalin, mainly in Siberia and north-central Kazakhstan. Used to punish both political dissidents and criminals, they gained worldwide recognition through the publication of Alexander Solzhinitsyn's novel *The Gulag Archipelago* in 1973.

academy in 1962. During my time at the Military Academy, in the somewhat more relaxed Khrushchev era, I was finally permitted to join the Communist Party – something I did only because I knew that it would be necessary for me to get a good position. Marina, Lena and I now began another round of wandering through the territory of this great multiethnic country. I was reassigned to the Zakarpatsky Military District as an assistant commander of a technical support unit located on the outskirts of the town of Vladimir Volynsky, a small town between Brest and Lvov in Western Ukraine, very near the Polish border and not far from Rokitno. The commander of the unit, Captain Ilin, was an alumnus of my military academy. Our unit was basically a regional storage facility responsible for supplying the troops with all the necessary fuels and lubricants as well as pure alcohol for aviation. I was responsible for the technical and technological aspects of storage.

When I found myself back in Western Ukraine, the memories of my childhood came rushing back. The dialects and little local traditions reminded me of the wonderful and the terrifying years I had spent here. And yet I had no desire to visit Rokitno, the town where I was born, spent my childhood, got my Jewish education and, more significantly, witnessed so many horrors. Instead I tried to block my feelings and emotions. I channelled all my energy into my work and my family. I was proud to be a Soviet army officer and I took my duties seriously. Even now, however, I was never able to entirely lose my sense of disappointment in doing a job that didn't require me to use any of the training I had worked so hard to acquire at the Suvorov Military School.

Intrigue Rears Its Unwelcome Head

Given the prevalent tensions of the Cold War, perhaps it should have come as no surprise when the fragile tranquility of our private lives was rocked by a major international event – the Cuban Missile Crisis of 1962.[1] As anxiety about the possibility of war with the United States mounted, our district started drafting many men into the military and our unit received new recruits daily. We now trained to be ready to build a pipeline to supply our troops with oil. There was a strong sense of panic in the streets, with crying women and children sending men off to the army, but there was little information about exactly what was happening. It reminded me of the beginning of World War II. Some of the units in our division were sent to Poland and Germany, but my unit stayed put. Then, thanks to the persistence and brinksmanship of the president of the United States, John F. Kennedy, this period of extreme stress and uncertainty came to an end.

Despite the upheaval on the world stage, life in the little town of Vladimir Volynsky was very dull and monotonous. My work in military storage was routine, Marina worked as a doctor in a small hospi-

---

1 The Cuban Missile Crisis, one of the major confrontations of the Cold War, was the October 1962 stand-off between the Soviet Union and the United States over missiles that the USSR had based in Cuba. It is usually seen as the time the two superpowers came closest to nuclear war. For more information, see the glossary.

tal and Lena attended kindergarten part-time. For Marina and me, my period of service in this town consisted mainly of military business, running errands such as "finding" food products, or wood and coal for heating, by trading and working around restrictions and short-ages, and the frustrating search for a reliable nanny for Lena. It was very difficult to find nannies who weren't alcoholics or psychological-ly unstable – that was our reality. Marina's father, Aaron Grigorievich, helped us with Lena a great deal and his visits were a real holiday for us. It was a pleasure to spend time in the company of this intelligent man. There were days when we'd go to the forest to pick mushrooms. There were so many white mushrooms that even without wearing his eyeglasses Aaron Grigorievich was able to pick a whole big bucket of them. These trips reminded me of the time when I was trying to survive in the forest eating these abundant mushrooms.

As it happens, Vladimir Volynsky was one of the first places to welcome the Jews who had flooded into Eastern Europe to escape the Spanish Inquisition.[2] Before World War II, two-thirds of its popula-tion had been Jewish, but only three or four of those Jews had sur-vived the war. Living there we met those few Jews who remained, as well as the families of other Jewish military personnel. Life in the military demanded the flexibility to adapt to different types of condi-tions and all kinds of relationships, especially for Jews.

My professional and personal life was moving along without in-cident when suddenly, in 1964, everything turned upside down: I re-ceived an order to report to Captain Odarchenko, the chief regional of SMERSH, the counterintelligence branch of the Committee for State Security better known as the KGB.[3] SMERSH was the branch re-

---

2 In 1492 Ferdinand and Isabella of Spain decreed that all Jews in Spain should be either converted to Christianity or expelled from Spain. Many fled to Turkey and North Africa, but some also made their way to Russia and Poland.

3 The Committee for State Security, or KGB, functioned as the secret police for the USSR. The organization was known for its cunning and brutality in persuad-

sponsible for ensuring security in the Soviet military. I was mystified by this summons because I was sure that there was nothing questionable in my military record. I was ordered to report to the office alone, without telling anyone where I was going or letting anyone see me, and these instructions alone instilled fear and uncertainty in me.

In what turned out to be the first of several encounters with this horrible Soviet organization, Odarchenko named various Jewish officers and asked if I knew them. He asked about one in particular, an assistant commandant of the antiaircraft artillery regiment who had been accused of losing a secret map during a field training session. I had never heard of this officer or this story and said so. After this, Odarchenko began asking me about my family history. He asked what I knew about my brothers and flashed several pictures at me that I didn't recognize and could barely see. He asked me to go home and recall "everything," and to this day I'm not sure what he meant by that. I was ordered to return the following night after dark. When I got home my only concern was for my brothers who lived in Israel and with whom I had no means of communication. For all that, Odarchenko's demeanour throughout the meeting had been pleasant, even friendly. But I still had no idea why I had been called in.

The next day I went to Captain Odarchenko's office late at night as ordered. This time his manner was more aggressive and threatening. First of all I was told not to tell anyone anything about our conversations. Secondly, he ordered my wife to report to him the following day as well. During our conversation I told him that I had had three brothers, that one of them had been killed by the Germans and that I had lost touch with the other two long ago. My wife had a very brief conversation with him the following night and signed a paper stat-

---

ing or intimidating people into giving evidence against or spying on friends and family. The name SMERSH came from the acronym for Smert Shpionam (Death to Spies). For further information, see the glossary.

ing that she would not tell anyone about any of our meetings with
SMERSH agents.

A few days later I was again told to see Odarchenko. This time
he showed me the cover of a file for a new case under investigation.
The name on the cover wasn't mine – it was "NOV," which I realized right away referred to my best friend from the Suvorov Military
School, Novik Sidorov. After another few days, I was asked to report
to Odarchenko yet again and this time he told me that my brother
Samuel's wife, Chaya, was coming to Moscow and that I should take
my family to see her. Apparently the Soviet authorities suspected that
she was an Israeli spy who was coming to meet me because I was a
captain in the Soviet army. I was so afraid of the consequences that
I tried to avoid meeting my sister-in-law at all, saying that I was sick
– which I actually was at that moment – with a high temperature of
about 39 degrees Celsius.

In reality, I was terribly torn. On one hand, I understood that this
meeting with my sister-in-law wouldn't be private and we wouldn't be
able to speak freely. Even without the involvement of SMERSH on my
end, as an Israeli her every move would be monitored.[4] On the other
hand, the truth was that I really wanted to meet her and hear about
my brothers. But perhaps most of all, I wanted to do whatever I could
to get rid of my constant fear that SMERSH might come around again
messing up my life. So, when the SMERSH fabricated a telegram saying that my wife's parents were sick and that it was urgent that we go
to Moscow – thus providing me with a cover for my absence from
work – I agreed to cooperate. This telegram had been authorized and
validated by a local doctor so that even my immediate superior at
work, Ilin, didn't know about the real reason for our trip. Prior to our

––––––––––––––––––––

4 Foreign visitors to the USSR at this time were routinely monitored by internal
   security; their movements were usually controlled by the state-run Intourist
   organization that routinely assigned a "keeper" to supervise foreigners travelling
   inside the Soviet Union.

departure to Moscow we also received a letter from my in-laws telling us what we already knew – that Chaya was coming to Moscow. They said that Aunt Roza had written to them about it from Birobidzhan.

A strange detective story now began to unfold. My final instruction from Odarchenko was to meet a KGB agent in a park in a neighbourhood called Fili as soon as we arrived in Moscow. The morning of our arrival, I did as I was told and met with a KGB major. He instructed me to listen carefully to everything Chaya said and to report every word back to him. I was ordered to accept any books or other printed material she offered to me and then to hand them over to him as well. He also told me I should not to wear my army uniform when I met her. I asked him if I could bring flowers and he replied, "Affirmative."

Chaya was staying at the Cosmos Hotel with her tourist group. I was given permission to bring Aaron Grigorievich along as my Yiddish interpreter for this emotional meeting. I had purposely neglected to tell the authorities that I could speak Yiddish perfectly myself – that would have made them even more suspicious.

The long-awaited day of the meeting finally came. I was very nervous. My desire to meet this woman who was a living link to my long-lost brothers was mixed with fear because I knew we were being watched and that anything could happen. Like everyone in the USSR I knew only too well what the KGB was capable of. Aaron Grigorievich and I bought a bouquet of flowers and went to the Cosmos Hotel where we met Chaya and went for a walk. The meeting was very tense. Our conversation was translated from Yiddish into Russian and back. I could tell that Chaya saw the fear in my eyes and didn't understand why it was there. To this day she still cannot fathom the way the Soviet system made us feel and understand why I didn't just speak Yiddish with her. She told us about her family and asked us about ours. We, of course, boasted about how wonderful our life was in the Soviet Union even though we ourselves didn't believe it. But that was our survival reflex under dictatorship. I couldn't let go of my fear. The next day we had a second meeting in Gorky Park. Chaya brought us presents, which, of course, we had to report to the KGB. As with our first meeting, all my thoughts were focused on my fear and the strangeness of this encounter. I had no idea how it would end for me.

When I returned to my unit in Vladimir Volynsky, I had to keep the real reason for my trip to Moscow secret, even from my immediate superior. But soon I was called in again by SMERSH, this time for a rather long interrogation about my meeting in Moscow conducted by Captain Odarchenko and several other SMERSH officers from the town of Rovno. The conversation started out gently, with praise for my service achievements, but the tone gradually shifted to threats and blackmail. They demanded to know the "truth" about my sister-in-law. I had nothing to hide – the truth was that Chaya had visited for only one reason: to see me and say hello from my brothers.

Captain Odarchenko, do you remember my visits to your office in Vladimir Volynsky? What about you, Colonel X? – I never did find out who you were. The former chief of SMERSH in the Luzk region, where are you? Do you remember how you and your faithful staff pressured me? Do you remember how during my mandatory meetings you threatened and blackmailed me? There were three of you and I was alone....

Right after Chaya's visit I did get a reprieve. For a while I continued to work as an assistant commander of the technical support unit, but then my commander, Ilin, was transferred to a teaching position at a military department of the Ivano-Frankovsk Oil and Gas Institute and I was asked to replace him. This was an unexpected promotion for me because, like anyone in the Soviet Union at this time who had relatives living abroad, I was considered suspect by the authorities and it was unusual that I would be put in a position of strategic importance. I accepted the offer and in my new capacity I began overseeing all the valuable military materials that we kept in the storage.

I had my own assistant, Senior Lieutenant Andrianov, the son of a military man from Brest. Andrianov was a rather tall guy, very bright and kind-hearted. We had a good relationship right from the start. In our unit we also had a lieutenant in charge of classified information, Sergeant-Major Medkov, and a laboratory chief, as well as civilian staff that included storage supervisors, lab assistants, workers, drivers, a dog-breeder and a full crew of firemen.

I worked hard to make sure that my storage was the best in the division and I succeeded. I demanded discipline from everyone, but I also made every effort to beautify and better our territory and its surroundings. For the first time I undertook a construction project, initiating the building of an indoor garage for the vehicles kept on reserve for urgent mobilization. Any construction project in the USSR faced challenges at this time – mainly a lack of building materials – and I once again had to use my resourcefulness to "find" what we needed. I managed to get the garage completed.

During annual inspections the administration of the Zakarpatsky military district noticed how I had changed the organization and operation of my storage facility and acknowledged the enhanced efficiency of the oil-supply system. As time went by, I gained the respect of the people in charge of both the division and the district. Yet I couldn't help but wonder why I had been promoted to a lieutenant colonel's position when I was only a captain and why I was kept in this capacity for eight years. It was unheard of!

Although my work routine was somewhat tedious, I had a good relationship with my staff. My assistant and I often went fishing, celebrated holidays together and I once went to visit his parents in Brest. We hired Natasha, a young woman with a technical education, as our new lab assistant and it wasn't long before Andrianov started to frequent the lab. Soon Andrianov was having an affair with Natasha while his wife, Shura, began an affair with the second secretary of the Party district administrative committee, who also happened to be my next-door neighbour. These romantic intrigues soon turned into a disaster. The first secretary of the district administrative committee found out about what was going on and called me into his office, suggesting that Andrianov be transferred to a different unit. This signalled to me that the military district administration had learned about it as well.

Andrianov was indeed transferred and his family moved to another town. I later heard that he had managed to maintain a long-distance affair with Natasha. Andrianov's transfer was a big loss for me. He was an honest, approachable man who always treated me with respect and had defended me more than once against personal slander. Once when I was away on a family vacation, for example, a military tribunal team came to investigate an accusation that I was engaged in illegal activity. I was accused of spending government money and selling gas and oil equipment and other materials from the storage. I later found out that these ridiculous accusations had been made up by one of the drivers on the fire-squad who was also a secret KGB agent. In my absence Andrianov had defended my honour tactfully and with factual proof.

There is another noteworthy incident that involved Andrianov and his lab assistant lover. During the famous Six-Day War in Israel,[5] when I was once again on vacation, the wife of Sergeant Major Medkov wrote an open letter accusing me, a Soviet army officer, of raising funds to support Israel and even communicating with the Israelis using state radio transmitters! She distributed this letter in town and began collecting signatures against me. She asked Natasha to sign, but she refused and immediately told Andrianov about the letter. He called me right away and came to visit the next day. He told me the news over a bottle of cognac in a restaurant. I broke into cold sweat because I knew what such claims could lead to. As it turned out, other

---

5   The Six-Day War (June 5–10, 1967) was fought between Israel and the armies of Egypt, Jordan and Syria, which were then aligned with the Soviet Union. For more information, see the glossary.

people had also refused to sign this petition against me and were angry with my accuser; her campaign against me led nowhere. Still such accusations kept me alert and ready for any attack, any consequence. In this atmosphere all I could do was maintain my high standards at work and try to stay calm.

Strange as it may seem, it was during the Six-Day War that I was finally promoted to the rank of major after an eight-year delay. Three other officers who oversaw other fuel and lubricants storage facilities were promoted as well. In another interesting twist, the news was announced at a training session for all the district officers in leadership positions that focused on analyzing the outcome of the Six-Day War. The presenters evaluated the military forces and tactics of both the Israelis and the Egyptians. Egypt's military and material resources were judged to be significantly better than Israel's, but Israeli tactics were considered to be superior. Israel had mobilized its troops much faster than even our district during emergency drills.

When my colleagues at the training session found out about the promotions, we decided to celebrate the additional epaulet stars of all four of the newly promoted officers according to military tradition. This tradition is called "washing the stars" because the new epaulet stars are placed at the bottom of a large glass filled with vodka and the officer has to drink it all, bottoms-up, to get his stars. I was just preparing to drink my vodka when I was told, much to my surprise and dismay, that my new rank had not been approved. No explanation was given. At that very moment I realized that my military career had reached a dead end.

I returned to my unit knowing that my fate had been decided and was in the hands of the KGB. After that, things happened fast. Without any explanation I was ordered to report to district headquarters to meet the chief of human resources, Major General Usov. Our conversation was not friendly – out of the blue he asked me how old my parents were and when I said that I didn't know exactly, he shouted at me, saying that even his three-year-old granddaughter knew her grandfather's birthday. I thought that I would end up being reassigned to Mongolia.[6]

Shortly after returning to my unit, I was called in for another meeting at district headquarters, this time to meet with the chief of fuels and lubricants. Once again, the purpose of the meeting was not explained beforehand. This time the conversation started with inquiries about my family history, after which I was reproached for hiding the fact that I had brothers who lived in Israel. After a short time another officer came in and was told to escort me back to Vladimir Volynsky, where he was to take over the unit. The handover of the unit, including all its materials and documentation, was rushed, breaking all the rules of protocol as well as the procedural rules regarding the handover of secret documents. The normal procedure was to form a handover committee. Not this time. The whole affair took three days. I was given an honorable discharge on the basis of a scheduled personnel layoff and went to register with the local military enlistment committee as a retiree. For the first time in my adult life, I was a civilian.

---

6 Mongolia, situated between China and the USSR, was a satellite of the Soviet Union during this period and reassignment to its inhospitable climate was often used as a punishment for officers and Party members who were being disciplined, reprimanded or simply kept away from assignments of significance or strategic importance.

The Events of an Unnatural Life

It was now December 1967 and a new and unfamiliar chapter in my life was about to begin. Marina and I decided to stay and live in Vladimir Volynsky where everyone knew me well, but I didn't know what I would do. I was soon offered a position as the chief engineer at a brick factory, but since I knew that three previous chief engineers were in jail for supposedly stealing state property, I was understandably afraid to take it. Nonetheless, I accepted the position and began learning the ins and outs of what was for me a new field. The majority of the factory workers were local Western Ukrainians. They still remembered life in capitalist pre-war Poland and I understood their mentality very well.

The director of the factory was a retired colonel who was a former commander of an antiaircraft regiment. He welcomed me warmly once he found out that I was a mechanical engineer and knew my way around heavy machinery. It didn't take long for me to learn my new trade and become a specialist in brick production. It was a fast-paced process. We used horses and wagons to pull hot bricks fresh out of the oven and then dried the bricks in the open under the sun. We oversaw other smaller branch factories that produced slacked lime[1] and bricks, and the director and I used to make trips to inspect

---

1 Calcium hydroxide, a mixture of lime and water that is used as mortar.

them. These visits always ended with heavy drinking. I knew that this job was a dead-end for me and would only be temporary, but I had to wait to make my next move. One interesting thing that I encountered on this job was workers who refused to work during religious holidays in defiance of deliberate instructions from the district Party administration. This is not something that I had seen before – certainly not in the military!

In early spring 1968, Marina and I decided to move to Moscow and, strange as this may seem, that seemingly ordinary plan affected our marital status. At that time the USSR had many complicated and paradoxical laws, some of which pertained to residency. For example, according to Soviet law, a person who was born in one place but had moved somewhere else could be banned from moving back to his or her hometown, particularly if the hometown was one of the bigger cities. We came up against that ban when we wanted to move to Moscow. But we discovered that if Marina was a single mother, she would be permitted to take our daughter – Lena was now almost seven – to live with her parents in Moscow. So, for the simple reason that we wanted to live somewhere else, we decided to get divorced. The plan was that I would stay in Vladimir Volynsky until Marina was re-registered as a permanent resident of Moscow, then I would join her there and we would marry again.

This was a very anxious time for us but in the end we were successful. I continued at my job at the brick factory in Vladimir Volynsky, counting the days until I got the go-ahead from my wife. As soon as I received word that Marina was registered as a permanent resident in Moscow and had started working, I quit my job and started packing. The director of the brick factory knew that I'd leave sooner or later. He understood that a dead-end job in the middle of nowhere was not for me and that I deserved more.

As I headed for Moscow in May 1968, I knew that I was facing many uncertainties – I was unemployed and would only be able to start looking for a job once I had my residency registration, which

I could only obtain by marrying a citizen of Moscow. Even then I would have to bribe the registration officials to get it – or at least to get it quickly. So, in order to move to a different city, I married the same woman twice – the first time in 1957 and the second time in 1968.

The next chapter in my saga was a three-month-long search for a job in Moscow. My search was complicated by the fact that most job applications now contained a question about relatives abroad; I would have to find an employer who wouldn't ask me about this. I finally found one and in June 1968 was offered a position as a senior engineer at the Special Design Bureau (SDB) of TransNeftAvtomatika (Trans Oil Automatics) at a salary of 120 rubles a month.

Another job application I had put in around this same time – to the scientific institute Neftezavody (Oil Factories) – was also accepted, but it turned out that the institute's Communist Party secretary, who was on vacation, didn't know anything about it. When he returned, I was called into his office and told that my application would have to be reviewed at a special hearing of the institute's Party committee. I assumed that this signalled a rejection for me and, sure enough, I was right. I decided to accept the offer from SDB TransNeftAvtomatika and started my new job on June 20, 1968.

In my new job I got to learn about a whole new area. By applying my usual diligence, I was promoted in due course to chief project engineer and later to assistant director of the standardization and pricing department. To help me successfully adapt to my new position, I enrolled in correspondence courses at the Institute of Standardization and Metrology in 1970. After completing these courses I began developing government standards for oil equipment production and usage.

During my time at SDB, I tried to keep a low profile and didn't aspire to being promoted to any higher positions than the one I had. A promotion would have required that I get a security clearance, which would, in turn, have exposed my secret – that I had relatives in Israel.

I was offered better positions several times, but each time I came up with some excuse to decline the promotion.

One of my duties at SDB was to conduct the so-called *politinformatsiya* sessions with young employees who were members of the Komsomol (Communist Youth League).[2] This generally involved telling them about local, national and international political events. During these sessions I usually just recited excerpts from newspapers clippings and added some humour, but avoided political jokes.

As I've said, my main task at work was to create various government standards. Each new standard that conformed to new technology regulations made the SDB eligible for monetary premiums – ten to 350 rubles extra for many people, especially for the chief engineer and the director of the SDB, who usually got the largest amounts. Then the money trickled down to those who actually worked hard to create the new standard. It was an interesting process that brought me in contact with people from different industries, and the standards review process always included drinking with the people in charge approving it. When I wasn't developing new standards at the SDB, I inspected other factories for compliance with existing government standards. During these review trips I encountered many cases of noncompliance and, even more frequently, deliberate misconduct or corruption. Such scheming was a way of life under the Soviet system.

In the early 1970s, Jews began to emigrate to Israel from the Soviet Union. Although the government did their best to silence dissent and deny exit visas to Soviet Jews, rising protests inside the USSR, growing international pressure and the beginnings of a thaw in the Cold

---

2 Komsomol, the wing of the Soviet Communist Party for youths aged fourteen to twenty-eight, functioned as a means of transmitting Party values to future members. Members of Komsomol were frequently favoured over non-members for scholarships and employment and being a young officer in Komsomol was often seen as a good way to rise early in the ranks of the Party.

War eventually led the Soviet Union to crack open the door. About nine of my Jewish colleagues at the SDB, some of them very capable engineers, left between 1971 and 1974. By 1974 I knew the time had come for me to go too.

A series of events led up to my decision, but foremost among them was the emotional impact of seeing my brother again. In 1974, after thirty years of separation, I was finally reunited with Samuel when he and his wife, Chaya, visited Moscow from their home in Canada, where they had moved in 1967. My previous meeting with Chaya in 1964 had been complicated, full of excitement and fear. This time we were able to get together without the KGB monitoring us. We welcomed our dearest guests to our Moscow home and visited them at their hotel, the Savoy Berlin. My cousin Victoria – Aunt Roza's daughter – and almost all of my wife's relatives came to meet my family.

Getting permission to leave the Soviet Union would certainly not be simple and would take some time. There were legal restrictions on when I could apply to leave because I had had access to secret information while I was in the army – I was forced to wait until a certain amount of time had passed before I could emigrate. As far as I was concerned, however, the countdown had started the moment I was forcibly demobilized from the Soviet army.

During my 1974 visit with Samuel and Chaya we talked constantly about my prospective emigration everywhere we went, even while sightseeing in Red Square. We went over every aspect of this critical life decision but kept coming up against one major problem – Marina didn't want to go. This became a serious issue between the four of us. When Sam enthusiastically tried to persuade Marina that she and Lena should come to Canada with me, she interpreted what they said as propaganda and her reaction was so vehement that it scared Sam and Chaya. They not only stopped trying to convince her, they became hurt and angry and started counting the days until their departure.

From this moment on my life turned into a series of nightmares. I was determined that we would all leave together and asked my brother Natan for an official invitation for our whole family to visit Israel. He sent it immediately. Now it was Marina's turn to decide "whether to pack an umbrella or not" (a Russian expression meaning that she would have to make up her mind come what may). Since we had a family invitation, all we had to do now was to collect and file all the necessary paperwork. The main obstacle for me, as I've said, was that my security clearance from the army had to expire before I could file my immigration papers. Even before this, though, from the moment Samuel and Chaya left to go back to Canada, Marina insisted that she wasn't ready to make such a radical move. I was flabbergasted. I was convinced that given everything that she knew about my past, and everything that was obviously so wrong with our present situation, my wife would want to leave. But I was wrong. She looked for any excuse to delay the process.

In the face of my wife's stubbornness, we had endless, frustrating and exhausting conversations. These were some of the cruellest days of my life because I firmly believed that I couldn't stay in the Soviet Union, that after everything I'd been through I deserved a better life for my family and me. Most of all, I wanted to have the freedom to think and express myself and not be labelled and treated as a second-class citizen. I didn't want to constantly encounter antisemitism.

The emotional burden of those days, weeks and months was overwhelming – the stress was almost unbearable. Marina eventually made up her mind and refused to leave the Soviet Union, and she had the support of her parents and relatives in this decision. I was alone in my decision to leave. The daily battles between us finally led us to the question of divorce. Without a divorce I wouldn't be allowed to leave. During this period we fought late into every night and then every morning I got up and went to English-language classes. This nightmare lasted several months.

When Marina finally agreed to sign all the divorce papers in court, I thought that my suffering was over. Wrong again. The way that the court official characterized the decision we were making caused Marina to change her mind again, and the court date had to be postponed for another couple of months. This latest complication left me feeling desperate and out of control. The days dragged on and on, slowly and painfully. Still, I was determined to achieve my dream of leaving the Soviet Union, a country where there was no present and no future for a Jewish Holocaust survivor.

Luckily, because all of this happened during a period of political thaw, I was allowed to continue working at the SDB, although in a lower-ranking position.[3] I was demoted from chief design engineer and sector head and was now simply an engineer. Despite the stifling atmosphere at home I kept hoping that my family would decide to follow me. I was gravely afraid that if they didn't I would never see them again, that the Iron Curtain would forever be between us. To keep myself busy I enrolled in an English-language study group. We sang songs like "My Bonny Lies Over the Ocean" – although no one in our group knew exactly who among us would really be going "over the ocean."

Over time, fewer and fewer people attended the study group. The smaller group became more close-knit and we started revealing our common secret – that we had all applied or were planning to apply to emigrate – and sharing valuable information about dealing with the bureaucrats at the Office of Visas and Registration (OVIR). We heard stories about people who were denied permission to emigrate and especially about Jews who were struggling for the right to move to Israel. Information was sparse and sombre, which didn't exactly encourage those of us whose immigration documents were already in the system.

---

3 In the early 1970s, tensions between the USSR and the West began to ease and diplomatic and economic contacts increased – a period of thaw in the Cold War known as "détente."

To top it all off, I now began to have a very hard time at work. It began with my petition to resign from my membership in the Communist Party, which I had to do before I would be allowed to leave the country. At the local Party bureau hearing a PhD student named Zimbler, who incidentally was Jewish, asked me a treacherous question. "Why didn't you mention your relatives abroad when you applied for a position at SDB?" I replied that I hadn't been asked – there was no question about it on the job application. After a brief discussion the members of the bureau decided to pass my case to the district Party committee. A date was set for another hearing. These passing days felt like an eternity.

The district committee consisted of old Party hacks who routinely slept through meetings and didn't ask any questions. During my hearing the first Party secretary of the district dropped by and for some reason concluded that I was leaving the country "on a mission for the Motherland." I was successfully expelled from the Party and began waiting for news from OVIR. The atmosphere at work, now that everything was out in the open, turned grave. Alexandrov, the chief engineer of SDB, instructed the staff to completely ignore me. Colleagues who had once shown me great respect now shunned me as if I had leprosy.

Finally the day arrived! After about seven months of agonizing waiting, I got permission to leave the country where I had spent the best years of my life – part of my childhood and youth and the period of becoming an independent family man. I was leaving the country where I had known first love and where my only daughter was born. I had decided to sever all these ties and memories in order to fulfill a dream for my family and for myself. I was taking a superhuman risk and was not 100 per cent sure of its outcome, but I knew deep inside that I had to do it.

Those last weeks were the terrible. I was leaving home again but this time voluntarily, on my own, without any external interference. Oh, kind people, who can understand the cries of my soul? My heart was breaking and I felt as if I were an orphan again. I wanted to scream but there was no one to hear me. The world was deaf and empty and the people ... everyone was preoccupied with their own sorrows. No one had time for mine.

In the last days before my departure I still clung to the hope that my family would go with me, but that didn't happen. I eventually packed a small suitcase and left my home, leaving everything and everyone behind. Everything, everything, everything.... Thinking about it brings tears to my eyes even as I write these words. I drove to Sheremetyevo airport in Moscow, feeling utterly empty. Before I headed for the plane I said farewell to my wife and her mother, Rita Moiseevna. I wondered what Rita was thinking in that moment? Unfortunately, she didn't live long enough to see that I still loved her daughter greatly and that I hadn't taken these risks lightly or in vain.

Building a Future

As I sat on board the plane on that January day in 1975, en route to Vienna, I was completely distracted and unaware of what was happening around me until takeoff. When we reached cruising altitude I wanted to scream, "Stop the plane! I want to get off! I forgot my family!" But of course that was impossible. So I stared out the window, bewildered, watching the tiny lights passing below, the lights of a country and a life I had left behind. The plane wasn't crowded and most of the passengers spoke Russian. The first part of my journey, the flight to Vienna, took about two hours.

When we landed in Vienna we were met by representatives of Israel and of Hebrew Immigrant Aid Society (HIAS).[1] They asked me where I wanted to go and I said Canada. It had been easier to get papers to leave the Soviet Union if I said that I was going to Israel, but in fact I wanted to go to Canada to join Samuel. All those who weren't en route to Israel were put on a bus and taken to an inn run by a Polish Jewish woman named Bettina. She was a very crafty woman. She exploited the immigrants who stayed at her inn, buying their goods and mementoes for a pittance and selling them for a big

---

1 Founded in New York in 1881, the Hebrew Immigrant Aid Society provides aid, counsel, support and general assistance to Jewish immigrants. Since the early 1970s, HIAS has provided specific assistance to Jews emigrating from the USSR.

profit. She behaved like a queen and her name became legendary to the many Soviet immigrants who crossed her threshold.

I roomed with an immigrant from Kiev, a fellow bachelor – that's what I was now – by the name of Garik. All the new immigrants gathered in the Vienna HIAS office to fill out paperwork. Since I spoke several languages I was asked to help with the translation. One of the people I helped was an immigrant from Poland who had loaded up his car and come to Vienna with the intention of staying there permanently. He offered to show me around and so I saw much of that wonderful city. Numerous writers and artists have praised its splendours. I was particularly impressed by the cleanliness of its streets, the discipline of its citizens and the abundance of everything in its shops. One week is not enough to see such a great city, of course, and my time there flew by quickly. Soon, along with a group of fellow immigrants, I was given papers to travel by train to Rome, Italy.

When our group arrived at the Vienna train station we had very little time to board the train and this unpleasant experience reminded me of the hurried retreat of the Soviet troops and the Party elite from Rokitno. Everything was chaotic as people wrestled with bags and suitcases of various shapes and sizes. I had it easy since all I had was one small suitcase.

The whistle blew and we departed once again into the unknown. The train wheels played the same melody as they had on the night of my journey from Moscow to the Suvorov Military School in Voronezh. The night train sped past one station after another. I wondered if we had been sent on a night train to avoid possible terrorist attacks.[2] I couldn't fall asleep for thinking over and over about everything that was happening to me. I also felt tremendous responsibility since I had been chosen to be the leader of the group. I was to make

2   In the 1970s, during the time that Alex Levin was in Italy, the left-wing militant group the Red Brigade (Brigate Rosse) was actively carrying out sabotage, kidnappings and assassinations.

sure that we all got off at the right station not far from Rome, where the HIAS buses would be waiting for us.

The scheduled stop there was very brief and we had even less time to get off the train than we had had to get on it. Suitcases and bags were tossed out the windows and suddenly awoken children cried. Nevertheless, everything worked out fine. We boarded the buses and headed for Rome.

In Rome we stayed in several boarding houses that were of a better quality than those in Vienna. Thus began my "Roman holiday." We could only stay in these boarding houses until HIAS in Rome finished processing our paperwork. After that we had to find our own housing. After taking advice from those who came before us, we found housing in Ostia di Lido, a small town on the Adriatic coast about thirty kilometres from Rome where the prices were considerably lower. I was lucky to find housing fairly quickly. My apartment was on Triremi street, right on the border between what my fellow immigrants called the communist and capitalist parts of town.[3] Garik, my roommate from Vienna, joined me again. I immediately threw all my energy into studying English seriously, taking the train to Rome for classes every day. I knew how important these lessons were because my knowledge of English would determine my success in the New World.

Modern Italy is one of the most interesting European countries, thanks to its geographical location, historic past, ancient culture and its role in today's Euroepan cultural and political scene. But having found myself in this wonderful country, all I could think about was my family. I held onto my faith in the triumph of reason and believed that we would eventually be together again. After every English class I would rush to the Ostia post office to call Moscow or to send a small

---

3 Ostia di Lido is a port for the city of Rome. Via delle Triremi divides the functioning port part of Ostia from the shopping and restaurant quarter.

care package that I had put together with savings from our small allowance from HIAS.

I ended up staying in Rome for nine months. After school and on weekends I roamed the city, indulging in its cultural riches. During this time I also had a chance to see most of Italy's famous sites and learned a lot about its wonderful people. I visited such places as Tivoli and the archeological digs in Ostia, magical Florence and Venice. I was greatly impressed with Italy and its people. Since the end of the war, the Italians had achieved so much socially and economically and all without the Soviet-style productivity rushes, competitions and mass mobilizations that we had known in the USSR, relying instead on their diligence and free will.

I not only pursued my English studies diligently but also attended every single HIAS lecture and class, as well as the meetings of a special group organized by HIAS director David Harris. He was a tall young man with an athletic build and we developed a really good relationship. Members of this study group rotated hosting duties, gathering in each other's apartments from the early evening to midnight with tea and cookies served over conversations in English about different topics. David had picked the members of the group himself and it included quite an interesting mix of people from different cities across the Soviet Union.

While I was in Rome awaiting my papers to Canada, Samuel paid me a visit, as did my oldest brother Natan, who came from Israel especially to celebrate what was, understandably, an emotional family reunion for the first time in thirty-three years! During our meeting we talked about our family who had been destroyed by the Nazis and their local supporters, and about my family in Moscow. Natan couldn't understand why my wife and daughter hadn't come with me since he had invited all of us. But immigration is a complicated psychological and physical process and I tried to explain that it was hard for Marina as well.

By fall 1975, my Roman holiday was finally coming to an end.

The screening process for immigration to Canada was very thorough and it was time for my medical evaluation and interviews with the Canadian consul. These procedures made me anxious, but at least I now truly believed that I would soon be in Canada. I could not help but think of the words written by the famous Russian poet Vladimir Vysotsky about Canada:

> This country is blessed by God,
> An Eldorado still not found –
> It's so funny – for here it is.
> Welcome to Canada! Welcome to Canada![4]

On October 28, 1975, I landed in this blessed land, in Toronto, Ontario. After getting through immigration at the airport I found myself in my brother Samuel's arms – after more than thirty years we were finally reunited for more than just a visit. Samuel's whole family was there to greet me. For the first time in my life, I got into a limousine and we drove along Yonge Street to my brother's house. It was evening and this wonderful street was full of neon lights and different shiny signs that I couldn't quite make out just yet. My only regret was that Marina and Lena couldn't see this beautiful display with me. And, as if it wasn't enough, the next morning I woke up in a luxurious house at 4 Shenston Street. I felt that I was in a dream – the kind you don't want to wake up from!

It was hard to believe that after everything I'd been through, happiness was still possible – and yet it was.

On my first day in their home my sister-in-law Chaya prepared dinner for all of us. How wonderful the food tasted! We talked endlessly, jumping from one topic to another. It seemed as if there couldn't possibly be enough time to discuss everything. Finally I was

---

4 Vladimir Vysotsky (1938–1980) was a Russian actor, writer, singer and poet whose underground songs about frustration with aspects of day-to-day life resonated with people in the USSR.

so exhausted that I had to go to bed. I was so wired with excitement that I thought I wouldn't be able to fall asleep. Surprisingly – or perhaps not – I passed out within minutes.

Toronto is a city that is spread out over a large area, and when I arrived in 1975 the Greater Toronto Area had a population of about 2.75 million. The city itself was only a couple of hundred years old so, by European standards, everything looked quite new. Then, as now, the real charm and strength of Toronto was in the many neighbourhoods that make up the city. I immediately felt very much at home with the strong work ethic of so many other immigrants like myself.

My first morning in Toronto marked the first day of my new life in a new house in a new country. I spent the first week filling out all the necessary paperwork to get government medical insurance and social insurance numbers. Then I registered with the local Jewish Immigrant Aid Society (JIAS) and enrolled in an English-as-a-second-language course at Seneca College.[5] My class of mostly Soviet immigrants met daily.

Within two weeks I realized that the level of this class was too low for me and I found a more advanced class at Humber College. This group consisted mostly of immigrants from India whose English was quite good, especially their written English, with two people from Israel and myself. Now I had no one in the class to speak Russian with whether I liked it or not. I was a very active member of the class despite my many mistakes, especially in my writing. I was determined to learn the language as soon as possible so I could look for a job, preferably in the engineering industry.

Career counsellors at Humber College helped students to search for jobs. One day, a couple of weeks before the end of my three-month-long English course, I was asked to go to a career counsellor's

---

5   Founded in 1919 in Montreal, the Jewish Immigrant Aid Society has assisted Jews from Eastern European Jews escaping pogroms, Holocaust survivors and Bosnian refugees, as well as Jews immigrating to Canada from around the world.

office. He told me about a an opening for an industrial engineer at the Fruehauf Trailer Company. I went to the interview with great enthusiasm and, happily, got the job.

My brother's house, where I was still living, was far from my new job and I had to take three buses to commute to work. I decided that I had to get a driver's license to make this commute easier. When I started my new job, I quickly realized that I couldn't expect help from any of my coworkers and that I would have to learn everything myself. I studied whatever I could find about manufacturing trailers and the other products in my new company. The main function of my position was to develop standards of production for the various auto parts used in the car platforms, trucks and vans that the firm assembled. Most of the time I had to calculate and measure the time contractors needed to produce these parts and the time that was actually spent doing it.

I quickly learned about all of our merchandise, developed appropriate standards for their production, systemized the information and created a database that allowed me to efficiently answer questions posed by other departments. At the same time, I developed good relationships with my coworkers, managers and the unions. While working at this factory, I also prepared to take exams to confirm my Soviet diplomas and register as a professional engineer in Canada. Upon successful completion of the exams, I became a member of the Canadian Engineering Association.

I was hoping for a promotion at work, but Lady Luck didn't smile on me just then. When there was a vacancy for the position of technical department chief, it was given to someone with more seniority. I continued my work under the supervision of a fairly competent man, although he didn't have a college education and was not a professional engineer. Nevertheless, we had a nice relationship and he quickly recommended a salary raise for me that was approved. After three years with this company, however, I decided that it was time to look for a better-paying job. I needed more money to save up for my family, who I still believed would join me in Toronto one day.

I got in touch with a so-called headhunting firm – a company that recruits professionals for jobs. Through them I was offered a position as a senior industrial engineer at another company. The salary was considerably higher and I soon had another new job with a new set of coworkers and new challenges. This company produced technologies and know-how for the manufacturing and assembly of car-radio tuners and created mini-production lines to test the technology before launching mass production in Haiti, where the cost of labour was very cheap.

With great enthusiasm I studied every detail of the newly developed tuner. The most important thing for me was to learn all the terminology of the radio parts and the production process in English. To achieve this goal I took a radio tuner apart and glued its individual parts on cardboard posters with the name and serial number of each part written underneath it. Then I simply memorized the whole chart. The prototype for our tuner was a Japanese model that our engineers had tried to modify and somehow make cheaper. However, during the modification process they missed a tiny spring part and this omission caused the new model to fail all the tests. I discovered this missing link when I was memorizing the names of all the parts glued on my cardboard charts. My discovery fixed the problem and soon the project was successfully finished.

I lived with my brother for my first six months in Toronto, but eventually the time came to find my own home and live independently. I quickly found a one-room studio apartment that I furnished with a few pieces of furniture given to me by my brother and nephew. I was a lonely bachelor and all my thoughts were focused on getting my family to join me as soon as possible. I wrote endless letters trying to persuade Marina that she had to take this step for the sake of our daughter's future.

I continued to work hard and save money to buy my own house. In my free time I started studying the real estate market. One day in 1978 my nephew told me about a new housing development being built near the intersection of Steeles and Bathurst streets. The site was at the very northwestern edge of the city in a suburb called Thornhill. They were selling houses in progress in that area. After two visits to the real estate office I made an offer on one of those houses and put down a deposit of $12,000 from my savings. The house cost $60,000, so I had to get a mortgage.

Although it may seem strange, I had to learn what a mortgage was and how it worked because it was completely unfamiliar to me. There was no such thing as a mortgage in the Soviet Union's socialist economy. While the house was being built I waited impatiently for news from Moscow and continued my hard work to pay off the mortgage more quickly. To secure a better salary, I changed jobs again and took a position as a manufacturing engineering manager at another company.

In a New Country

After five years of separation and uncertainty my family finally made the decision to come to Canada. It was our daughter, Lena, who finally turned the tide. Lena had graduated from high school with a gold medal and should have been welcomed with open arms to any top university of her choice, but instead was experiencing the same kind of discrimination in being admitted that I had faced in the Soviet Union. Marina realized that for Lena to truly have the opportunities that she deserved, they would have to leave the USSR. I filed all the paperwork and waited for a happy family reunion that finally took place on the joyous day of January 31, 1980. Samuel and his family came with me to the airport.

After the regular customs check Marina and Lena were finally in my arms. This time, however, I was able to drive my family to our own house. Before their arrival, Samuel and his family, Natan, who was visiting at the time, and I had tried to make the house as comfortable and cozy for my family as we could. We got new furniture, dishes and various little homey things that would contribute to their comfort and ease in this new environment. I must confess that I also wanted to impress them with my security and relative material wealth.

My dream of many years had now come true. My family was finally with me in the fresh, affluent land of Canada and we could start life anew. During the first few days we filled out all the paperwork required of new immigrants. Since I'd already done that before we finished that part quickly. Now it was my family's turn to study hard. They enrolled in an ESL school and actively pursued the language. Lena, who by this time was eighteen years old, already had a solid base of English but had never had an opportunity to practice the language. Her goal was to get settled as soon as possible and apply to university. She applied to the computer studies department at York University in Toronto for fall 1980, and since she had graduated from high school with honours, she was accepted with the condition that she take additional language training. Meanwhile, Marina diligently continued to study English at George Brown College.

That same year I started a new job as a production manager in another factory. My responsibilities and salary grew annually. Every job I have ever done has had its positive and negative sides. But the most important thing to me at this time was that my material and financial status continued to grow stronger and that I acquired local experience in different industries. It was always a source a pride for me to be able to say proudly in all my job interviews after my first one that yes, I had Canadian work experience. In contrast to my experience searching for jobs in the Soviet Union, nobody in Canada ever asked me about my ethnicity or age because it was illegal to do so. In Canada I no longer faced a "paragraph five denial" of employment. And no employer ever asked me where my relatives lived!

Our life in Canada gradually grew to feel more and more normal and comfortable. This simple fact of having my family with me in this blessed country after years of struggle and suffering proves that if you fight for your future you can indeed attain happiness. Marina and I had our third wedding on October 3, 1980, in Toronto. Of course life in Canada is not always as smooth as some people across the ocean might perceive it. But the most important thing is that here one can truly sing the famous Soviet song that contains the words, "My native country is wide… Where everyone breathes so freely…." You have to do only one thing and that is to work diligently and with honesty – and so I did.

Working as a production manager I not only gained experience in launching new products, working with strong unions and a multicultural staff, but also participated in the hiring and firing process. My decisions were often both technical and personal and always focused on ensuring timely completion of high-quality orders. I worked hard and in due course I became successful.

Despite my evident progress, or perhaps due to it, I also acquired some enemies in this factory who didn't want me to succeed and tried to make it impossible for me to do so. At one point I wanted to make changes to the group dynamic and work habits that had existed before my time because I felt that they were hurting our productivity. The result was that I got fired for no reason whatsoever. I believed that such termination was not justified and I went to court to fight it. The court awarded me a settlement. The monetary compensation was of little importance to me. What was important was that my position was validated. I also think that it was an important legal case because it showed that an immigrant could sue a multimillionaire owner of a company and win. When I compare this to my difficult experiences in the Soviet Union, I often wonder, Is this for real?

Having lost that job I was committed to finding a new one, but this time I was more confident and my English was much better. Shortly thereafter, in 1981, I was offered a position in the oil industry, which was much closer to my education and experience in the Soviet Union. After the initial interview in Toronto I was called in for the second interview in Calgary. I flew out there with great enthusiasm. On this trip I saw the magical Rocky Mountains for the first time. It was breathtaking! I got the position, but my family didn't want to move again. I agreed with them and returned to looking for work in Toronto.

In January 1982 I was offered a position as a corporate plant engineer in one of the largest laundry services in North America. I got a raise after a year and thought there was no reason to worry, but life sometimes throws you a curve. My boss was a Hungarian refugee who had climbed the company ladder all the way to the top without an education in engineering. He decided to hire a recent college graduate, the son of a friend, instead of me for a certain position. One day, my boss simply handed me a letter saying there were no more projects for me to work on. Since I had had some experience fighting injustice, I sued the company for wrongful dismissal. Such struggles in life are tough, but if you're fighting for your right to be treated fairly, they actually give you strength. Once again I prevailed and was awarded another financial settlement.

Armed with Canadian work experience and knowledge of the judicial system, I decided it was time to open my own business and not slave for someone else. I got my real estate license in 1983 and started a new chapter in my work history that can best be described by the Russian proverb, "It is the wolf's legs that keep his belly full." Real estate taught me a lot about human relationships such as loyalty, honesty and ethics and that everyone can have a positive and negative side. But the national real estate market went down significantly at this time, so I decided to get a job as a plant manager at a food-machinery engineering company, designing equipment for bakeries.

In 1985 I began working as a real estate sales associate and had a rather successful year. But this type of business didn't really interest me and so I decided to invest in buying land and building housing developments. Working with a business partner, Vito Marchese, we set up our own construction company called Alvi Homes in 1987. We started out with just two houses, but the construction and sale of both houses was extremely successful. Now that we had experience in construction, we found a customer who wanted his house completely renovated and enlarged. Our expertise in house construction grew and we expanded our project to ten houses. My partner and I did very well on that endeavour. After that success I let up somewhat on my commercial projects. I still worked as a builder, but it became a little easier and the pressure wasn't as great.

Around this time, in 1991, we prepared to welcome my wife's sister, Vera Zeitlina, and her family of five to Canada. Convincing her to move had taken years of persuasion and a reconnaissance mission by Vera when she had attended Lena's marriage to Jack Halpern on March 13, 1988. Then later her husband and daughter visited with us as well. Finally, we got a letter from Vera saying that the family was ready to immigrate to Canada. The family arrived in Toronto on December 27, 1991.

I had achieved a degree of financial stability in Canada that I had never thought possible. I had worked very hard all my life, mostly to survive in the best way I could. There was satisfaction in this, of that there can be no doubt. But my personal history now challenged me more and more and I wished, as I had wished when I was only a boy, that I could do something to help others prevent a horror like the Holocaust from ever happening again. They say that those who ignore their own history are destined to relive it. I was haunted by the thought of this and now that I was essentially retired, I finally did something about it.

I began to work for Holocaust-education organizations, which meant breaking my longstanding silence about my own terrible experiences. This was quite difficult. It took effort and a certain kind of courage to talk to strangers about what happened to me during the war. Nevertheless, I became a public speaker, going into schools and other organizations to share and to inform. I knew it was important for the younger generation to learn about these events from someone with firsthand experience of the Holocaust, to hear not only about the horror but also about how a few of us had been able to survive.

In the course of a varied and sometimes difficult life I had become a rather successful entrepreneur. Although it may not be the rags-to-riches story of the century, to me it all seems remarkable. I was a little boy when the home and security and love that a family can provide were brutally taken from me. I can't help but relive my time in the forest, time that gave me, paradoxically, a spiritual side. Whenever I turn inward, I see, in my mind's eye, the towering trees of the forest. I also see the wolves, their evil eyes glowing in the dark.

Whatever career success or long-sought-after security that I have achieved is, I believe, the result of a life that has been simultaneously meaningful, challenging and – at times – seemingly hopeless. I am satisfied with what I have and what I have accomplished. I learned firsthand how important my family is to me. At the very least I can positively say that there is some order to this life. No one need finally despair.

Epilogue: Our Journey to the Places under the Yellow Stars

When I began speaking to people about what had happened to me and my family during the war years in Europe, and as I began to relive the painful memories of my childhood, I became more and more desperate to find answers to my questions and a way to ease my pain. I was now a Canadian citizen, living a world away from where I grew up and I felt as if I were split in two. One part of me was empty and hurt and European. The other part was more whole and fulfilled and Canadian. Inevitably I began to think about returning to Europe to see the places where I had spent my youth in the hope that doing so might finally calm some of the desperate emotions churning inside me.

On one level I understood that visiting Rokitno in 1995 would be like visiting the museum of a lost civilization. I would be searching for a vanished Jewish world. The Polish and Ukrainian people continued to live there as they had for generations, but the Jews who had lived there for a thousand years have left no trace. Those of us who are survivors wonder if it is even possible to travel to that vanished world. Our childhood was stolen from us – would it be possible to somehow get a piece of it back? This idea drives many of us. By going back, perhaps we might discover some photograph or artifact, some witness of our loved ones.

Although I ached to return to Rokitno I also secretly resented the very idea of going back. For me, Rokitno has represented something that I can only call meaninglessness, a place that has haunted me with feelings of indifference rather than of passionate hatred and fear. But despite these difficult feelings, I knew on some level that I wanted very much to go. After many years of discussion and debate, my brother Samuel and I finally decided to make the trip. We not only felt that we should see our birthplace once more for ourselves, but also that we should see our childhood home for the sake of our families and, quite simply, for the entire generation that knows so little about what happened there.

We made inquiries about returning to the area and learned that there was an organization that arranged regular visits there. In 1995 we were fortunate to join a group of Israelis – survivors, their spouses, children and grandchildren – who also had roots in Rokitno. We would be part of a yearly pilgrimage organized by the Association of Former Residents (and their descendants) of Rokitno and its surroundings. With mixed emotions, Samuel, members of his family and I made our travel arrangements.

I arrived in Kiev, the capital of Ukraine, a few days before Samuel, his family and the Israeli contingent. I wanted to spend some time there with my former schoolmates from the Suvorov Military School in Voronezh, including, among others, Fred Zolotkovsky, Vladimir Beliaev and Boris Poliansky. Our reunion was very emotional and the conversation was stimulating – we talked about everything from our years at cadet school to the meaning of life itself.

We visited the infantry school in Kiev, the cemetery where Fred Zolotkovsky's parents are buried and in the evening visited Fred's cousin, Lena, who hosted a party for us. This party was in fine Russian tradition – lots of food, lots of vodka and lots of speeches about my visit and our friendship. The warm and nostalgic evening reminded me of our youth, our lost schoolmates and our teachers. In that spirit, I invited Fred to join us on our journey to Rokitno to learn about my childhood and he accepted.

Two days later Fred and I met Samuel and his family at the airport.

The group from Israel, having arrived earlier, was already en route to Rokitno by bus. Samuel, Fred and I, along with Samuel's family, divided ourselves into two cars and began the long drive to Rokitno, a journey of about 260 kilometres. On the way I talked to our chauffeur and Samuel talked to his children, telling them stories and sharing important information to prepare them intellectually and emotionally for their arrival in this almost mythic place. When we arrived we were welcomed by Nina Ivanovna Chiruk, former vice-mayor of Rokitno, and by the group from Israel. We were invited to a restaurant and then to the Dubok hotel.

After a short rest we began walking the streets of our town, starting at the railway station that hadn't changed in all these years. The cattle cars that were displayed as a memorial to those who were murdered by the Nazis were identical to those that had transported the people who were still alive after the shooting in the market square, among them my father. We walked to the ruins of our street – the same road we had taken to school before the war. We passed the railway crossing, we saw the bridge over the small river and we passed Mr. Nachtman's house, another place where we had picked juicy pears when we were small. Describing my life to Fred helped me to express some of my complex emotions. Fred was so moved by what I told him that he started writing poems about his feelings in sympathy.[1]

On the second day we went to a meeting with local government officials and heard a report about the development of the region. Some of the Israelis spoke about our reasons for coming back to the shtetl, how we wanted to show respect to the lost community and to visit the places where we had passed our childhood years.

On the third day we went to the newly fenced Jewish cemetery, where we found several new gravestones and many old ones. The new gravestones were of those Jews who had come to Rokitno af-

---

1 One of these poems is included in the appendices at the end of this volume.

ter the war and have since died. The only Jews still left in the town are the dead ones. We lit memorial candles and recited Kel Maleh Rachamim, the memorial prayer for the departed. We all now felt a strong connection to the past. Samuel and I searched the cemetery for our grandfathers' graves but we couldn't find them.

Not far from the cemetery is the mass grave containing the remains of people who were massacred in the market square or who were killed trying to escape by wartime collaborators for as little as one kilogram of salt. We held a memorial ceremony for them. It was a deeply meaningful moment; we all dissolved into tears. We draped the Israeli flag over the gravestones and recited the special Kaddish prayer, the mourners' prayer.

On the fourth day we went through the nearby village of Netreba to Okopy, in the area where Samuel and I and others had hidden in the forest. The Polish Catholic village of Okopy was completely destroyed by Ukrainian nationalists. Only the cemetery remains. One of the local people told us about what had happened there. He even knew about our hiding place deep in the forest, but explained that our dugout cave was now impossible to visit because it was filled with water. He also told us what happened to Ludwik Wrodarczyk, the local Polish priest, and Felicja Masojada, a Polish teacher, who had helped us during the war – that both of them had been brutally murdered. He also told us that Mrs. Masojada's son Edmund was alive and living in Warsaw.

Samuel and I remembered our long search for shelter when we wandered from village to village. After being turned away by many, Felicia Masojada, who lived on the outskirts of the village of Okopy, and Ludwik Wrodarczyk had given us temporary shelter, food and clothes. Now, hearing that her son was alive, we got in touch with representatives of the Polish Catholic church until we finally made contact with Edmund Masojada.

On the way back to the Dubok hotel we were invited to the high school to meet the teachers. Samuel's daughter Miriam David was particularly interested in the discussion there because she is a teacher in Toronto. Then we stopped at childhood home of Moshe Trossman – who was part of the Israeli group – where we could still detect the marks left by the *mezuzah* that his family had put on the door frame.[2]

On the fifth day we drove to Sarny, where 18,000 Jews from surrounding towns and villages had been murdered. We got off the bus near a football stadium – it has been built over the old Jewish cemetery. We crossed the train tracks and followed the road our people had walked to their own mass grave. In that grave were the remains of my father, along with his brother and sisters. This massacre is described in a book written by a survivor, Israel Greenberg, who managed to escape by hiding in a pile of clothing.[3] There are three memorials on the site, made of three mountains of bones covered with sand. On our visit we once again held a memorial ceremony.

We drove back to Rokitno and stopped at the market square. My brother tried to recreate the horrible day that our mother and brother were killed. He described to his children how families were separated, how one woman shouted a warning that a slaughter was about to happen, the chaos of the terrified crowd trying to run to safety. Then Samuel crossed the road and showed them the house that we ran to, where he had worked for the German officers. We all felt a chill feeling and Samuel's adult children were visibly affected. He told them how we had run away from that house, out the back door and under the railway cars that had been prepared for the whole community to be transferred to the Sarny pits. He described how we had run further into the bushes and into the dense forest surrounding our town.

---

2 A *mezuzah* is a small piece of parchment inscribed with verses from the Torah that is usually enclosed in a decorative casing and placed on the doorframes of homes of observant Jews.

3 Israel Greenberg (Afula), "Tearful Events," translated by Ala Gamulka, in *Rokitno-Wolyn* and *Surroundings: Memorial Book and Testimony (Ukraine)*, edited by E. Leoni (Tel Aviv, 1967), 282–287.

On our last evening in Rokitno, local government officials invited us to a dinner at a restaurant. While we were there, an intense rain began to fall. We felt as if the heavens were crying as our fallen were remembered. The table was set up with food and vodka. The orchestra greeted us with Ukrainian and Hebrew songs. It was Friday evening. We lit the Sabbath candles and prayed.

Appendices

כאַװער רויטאַרמייער

שיקע לעװינג

"Comrade Soldier of the Red Army" by J. Land in the original Yiddish (see opposite).

Comrade Soldier of the Red Army · J. Land

It is not the first time that people have asked, "Who are you, boy?"

He saw and endured so much that it would be too much for a grown man, and yet here and now he is addressed as "boy."

"Who are you, boy?"

~

It was a dark night in the forest. Autumn plucked leaves from the trees. Falling stars streaked across the sky, their tails illuminating the forest for a moment and then the light was quickly extinguished.

Fear enveloped him and shadows crawled. The wind whistled and was ready at any moment to pounce. Every tree seemed like a murderer and every branch a hand or a fist. He is nine and alone in the woods. His name is Shike Levin. What is he doing alone in the forest? He ran there to save himself. He escaped from his town. It is dark and it seems as if death is following him. He thinks that he hears guns being fired in the stillness of the night. He imagines that humans are hanging from the trees and Jews from his shtetl Rokitno are hanging on the doors of their houses. A fir tree with broken branches reminds him of his mother, with her hands folded, unable to cry because of fear and misfortune. She seems to stand over the father's dead body. Should the boy approach her? Should he come over to his mother and huddle close to her and tell her that he is afraid? She told him before her death, "Child, if you want to live, conserve your energy and run." The next moment it seems to him that his mother is hanging from one of the trees.

He stands pressed against a tree stump. He is cold and afraid to look around – perhaps he will cheat death. He begins to hear noises. It seems to him that he is surrounded by wolves who are looking for him. Could it be the same wolf from the stories that his mother told him? An entire way of life had disappeared at that moment. He feels that he has suddenly grown up – but the wolf is still a wolf.

He lies hugging the stump and drops into sleep. Rain, mixed with dew wakes him in the morning. He opens his eyes and quickly shuts them again. The rain gathers strength and the droplets from the branches urge his departure. He looks around trying to decide which way to go or whom to look for.

"Who are you, boy?"

Two armed men stand before him. They are observing him. They want to know how a small boy wound up in the forest. "Who are you?" He could tell much, but only tears come out. Quietly they search for an answer from the boy. They ask again, "Who are you? We are partisans." His crying increases. His salty tears reach his mouth and he manages to utter, "I am a Jew"

~

He lives and helps the partisans for a period of three years. After the shtetl Rokitno is liberated, Shike Levin leaves the forest and comes to town. During the three years he becomes older and taller. His black hair and worried eyes remain the same. He wore shoes made out of reeds and an old army cap on his head. His oversized pants and overused peasant shirt covered his body. He enters the liberated town wondering whom he would meet. Certainly no mother or father – perhaps an uncle, an aunt or a neighbour. Leaving the forest brings back the feeling of three years ago. He feels alone – the forest acted as his father. It protected him. Now the same loneliness wells up in him. The sun, as is its habit, searches the roofs of the houses. Shike Levin also searches the familiar streets of his childhood. Slowly he looks into every familiar house. He is no longer a twelve-year-old. Those years no longer exist for him. He is now a Red Army soldier.

An officer of the Red Army looks into his fearful eyes and asks him, "Who are you?" "Who am I?" A smile appears on Shike Levin's face. "I am a partisan!"

~

The same evening, Shike Levin becomes the Red Army mascot. He is given a bath, fed well and supplied with a military uniform, Together with his unit, Shike went through the whole of Poland until he reached the German border. He serves as a "gofer" for the unit and every soldier knows him as the kid who brings letters and parcels from the military post office.

The war ends in May 1945. One day in August, a young soldier of thirteen appears at our editorial office. The military uniform fits well and the boots are shined to lustre. His uncomfortable gaze reveals a pale gentle face. However, the military uniform makes him look more childlike. He looks around and wonders to whom he should address himself. I notice him and ask him, "Who are you, boy?" He looks at me seriously and grudgingly replies, "I am a Red Army soldier."

We become good friends and he explains that he arrived in Moscow recently to attend the Suvorov Military Cadet School.

"So you want to be a military man?" I ask.

"Definitely. The Germans tried to annihilate us. That's why I want to be a military man so that no one can ever do us any harm again.

If you should meet a thirteen-year-old soldier in uniform with the above description, do not ask him, "Who are you, boy?" You may address him as "Comrade Red Army soldier."

This article was originally published as "Khaver Royterarmeyer" in the Yiddish-language newspaper of the Jewish Anti-Fascist Committee, *Eynikayt* (Unity), in Moscow in 1945. It has been translated from the Yiddish by Lawrence Galmulka, BCom, MA (Eng). A reproduction of the original appears on page 122.

The following are speeches given by me, my brother Samuel and Fred Zolotkovsky on the occasion of our visit to Rokitno in 1995:

I will start by quoting a well-known Russian movie producer, Sava Kulish: "My generation is the last generation of the war, of children of the war. We are the last generation, with whom the facts, reality and personal knowledge about the wartime will disappear. Our childhood experience is also valuable for history, as valuable as the adults' memories of the war. Our bitter knowledge will disappear forever if we do not secure it in films, books, art."

My generation experienced a war at the most sensitive age, but in the fifty years that have passed we have all become adults. More than that, we have realized that the more we turn around and try to evaluate the past the truer it becomes. Only if we understand the past can we accept the present and anticipate the future that our children and grandchildren will experience.

Our children and grandchildren will live in that future. Without them we will not have a new generation. But it is very painful to think that the mistakes for which we paid so very dearly might be repeated fifty-four years after World War II, the war that destroyed millions of human lives.

Our families were caught in this big wave of history. In escaping from the Nazis we Jews of Rokitno hid in a dense Ukrainian forest and the mud of Polesie fields. We saw cruelty and kindness, hunger and cold, but youth and the will to live gave us the strength to survive. We have come together today to remember our parents, brothers and sisters. They were innocent victims. They didn't have the opportunity to develop their potential and see and enjoy the achievements of their children and grandchildren. For the sake of a peaceful future, the children of war cannot be silent!

Alex Levin
Rokitno, 1995

I was born seventy years ago, in 1925, in the town of Rokitno. I grew up and spent seventeen years of my life there. We lived a simple life. My father worked hard and we were poor. We were four children. I remember that some Fridays there was not enough food to prepare for the sabbath. In spite of it all we lived as a happy family with our parents. Suddenly, in 1942, we became orphans. We gathered in the market square where the Nazis and their collaborators began to shoot, to hunt the runaways and load them into the railway cars. They brought these cars full of people to Sarny where all of them were killed, including our father. He was murdered there, together with many others, without compassion.

From the loud screaming and crying in the market square that day, I saw the sky open up and I looked for our God to save us. It did not happen, and from then until now have I believed that such a God does not exist. My mother and my five-year-old brother did not escape into the forest and they found only death. My brother Sasha, who is here today, and myself did manage to escape into the forest. We struggled through a torturous path that is difficult to describe because I myself cannot believe how we were able to go through it. I remain troubled today with the question I asked then: Why?

I don't want to make this evening too sad, too emotional. I want to forget the past, but it is difficult. I tell you this story because my heart is aching and I cannot even cry – I have no tears left. I waited more than fifty years to come back to the place where I was born and reunite with my dear parents who are gone. I just had to finally unburden my heavy heart. I want to thank all those people who organized this trip, especially Yisachar and Moshe Trossman and all the others who helped. Thank you.

Samuel Levin
Rokitno, 1995

Memory is one of the valuable beginnings. In any situation there are opportunities that allow everybody to remain human in the full sense of the word. In these memorable days, we have visited the monuments of those who perished in August 1942 in Rokitno and Sarny. Your relatives and close friends were killed only because they were Jews. This is monstrous. This is frightening. This was a black and bloody page in our lives. One of the morals is that even horror and grief purifies us morally and in spirit. Without doubt all the victims, their incredible spirits and our memories of them bring us together and make us a more solid and harmonious nation. Do other nations not wonder about the people who survived that horrible time? The Jews who survived – we memorialize them as heroes – and we admire also the Ukrainians, Poles and White Russians who did not sell their souls to the devil. Under the German occupation they remained human. These are the thoughts and feelings that I want to express in my poems.

Fred Zolotkovsky
Rokitno, 1995

Jewish Cemetery, Rokitno, 1995

There it is, the old Jewish cemetery
Row upon row, and every weathered stone
Is a memory, and a plate of grief.
Yes, this place tells of executions, pogroms
And the fires of hate that were lit.
These are holy places, these graves
Of our ancestors.
Look here! A sister. Beyond! A brother
in clattered disarray. Unfindable
Parents and grandparents. Broken stones,
Scattered bones. Friends. All in one tomb now.
In time dust will consume it
And it will disappear anyway.
Great clouds are spreading low over the horizon

And the atmosphere is almost electric.
All of us here are pained and distressed.
On one of the stones we saw a Star of David,
But the name and date could not be read.
Just a stone erected through the centuries.
That stone represents thousands of years,
Forever it represents the faith of our fathers
And countless fathers before them.
That faith was never bent nor struck.
Change was not in our nature.
Obstinacy was always our protector.
This cemetery, this is our history.
It is God's hand.
Let us all stand around the graves today
And we will recite Kaddish
In memory of our fathers.
Maybe we will all be purified
without loud and significant words.

FRED ZOLOTKOVSKY, 1995 (translated from the Russian by Alex Levin)

The Inextinguishable Candles of the Holocaust

As Holocaust survivors we all came away from a tragic universe of death and destruction with scars that will never fully heal. We were strangers when we arrived on this continent. People looked at us with suspicion, wondering how we survived when millions of others had perished. In most cases we kept our memories to ourselves. The general public, Jewish and non-Jewish, didn't show any special interest in our past or our problems. The world wanted to forget the Holocaust and not be burdened by our tragic experience. It was the survivors who stood at the forefront and challenged the world to remember. We began the commemorations and memorial pilgrimages to the sites of the death camps and mass graves.

Even as we rebuilt our shattered lives in the New World, the slogan "Remember" was repeated loudly and clearly at every occasion, urging others to join in the sacred task of remembrance. But not many people celebrated our newly attained freedom. Our commemorations were mostly attended by survivors. We were the ones who understood Elie Wiesel's moving plea to survivors, his warning that if we forget, we, too, shall be forgotten.

We survivors have also recognized one group of people endowed with a unique humanity that qualified them as the conscience of the world: the Righteous Gentiles. Small in number and steadily dwindling, they are the beacon of light toward which all people, including us, should strive.

We survivors are the proof against the Holocaust deniers. We are the living witnesses to the past. And so groups of survivors organized themselves and took on the task of commemorating, documenting and educating people about the greatest calamity that befell European Jewry. A Holocaust survivor named Robert Engel from the Holocaust Centre of Toronto encouraged me to become a volunteer. I have devoted myself for more than eight years to speaking to students from religious and secular schools and to university students.

Whenever I speak to students, it is very rewarding to see their eyes fill with tears and compassion. They often give me warm hugs. I have received hundreds of letters each year from visitors to the Holocaust Centre and from the schools and libraries I have visited. I would like to share some of them:

Dear Alex,

We thank you for being so generous. You have given us a gift of knowledge and understanding of the Holocaust through your personal experience. We appreciate this rare opportunity, and we are truly honored to have you here. We will not forget, and we will tell your story, so that our children will also learn about the Holocaust.

Thank you from the bottom of our hearts.

Shana Brosyi,
Lisa Henneman,
Markham District High School

Dear Mr. Levin,

I was the girl who cried while you were telling us your story. I am writing to you because that day when you told your personal story you moved my heart.

Thank you for your strength in life and your knowledge of living. People of your nature allow people like me to want to enjoy life ever more because you made me see with my heart what people had to endure.

Dear Mr. Levin,

Thank you so very much for taking the time to speak to my students. We are so blessed to have met you. It was an honor, indeed. Just being in your presence was an honor. You are kind, compassionate and an amazing speaker with a beautiful sense of humour. You are indeed a survivor. We are blessed to have heard you speak. We learned so much from you and we will always remember you and your words.

God bless you, always.
Lina De Luca,
Teacher, York Memorial CI

Dear Mr. Alex Levin,

I know it's hard walking down "memory lane" because it's very painful. But I want to personally thank you for sharing your story with me. It was a privilege to be able to learn about history from someone who had been there…. Your story made me realize how lucky I am to be living in a peaceful world. Thank you very much. I am really happy that you now live here in Canada and was able to start a new life. God bless you and your family.

Gredaline Teves,
Father Michael Goetz Secondary School

Dear Mr. Levin,

The teachers and Grade 6 students from Bayview Glen Public School were most impressed with your talk. It is very important for young people to hear about the Holocaust at first hand, so they can hear the answer to the question, "Did it really happen?" from someone who lived through it. I can appreciate how hard it must be at times to re-tell events, but you obviously have the same conviction that the story must be told. It was good to see that some adults came along independent from the class to hear you speak, and what a surprise to see your confrère from the forest! I wish you the best of luck with your book.

Sincerely,
Sharon Philip, Supervisor, Children's Services,
Thornhill Community Centre Library

~

In 2002, I was asked to join the March of the Living college program as one of the Holocaust survivor participants. March of the Living is an international educational program that brings teenagers to many of the key sites where the tragic events of the Holocaust took place.

My mission in this difficult and sensitive task was a significant event in my history – to light the memorial candle, to keep the inextinguishable flame of the Holocaust burning. This was an opportunity for me to accompany students as they travelled through Poland and Israel, a once-in-a-lifetime experience during which I shared moments of sadness and joy that have created long-lasting bonds. After she returned home to New York from our trip, Samantha Peller wrote,

"I wanted to share a song I wrote a few months after returning from the trip about my experience in Poland. One of the concentration camps we visited, Majdanek, had a barrack that housed cage upon cage of shoes of Holocaust victims." The song, "Shoes," concludes:

> These little children have lost their shoes
> And lost their lives and yet,
> Their tiny little shoes remain
> shoes reminding us all to never forget.

The students who visited Poland have also shared with me the stories of their encounters with Polish young people, students from various universities.

These non-Jewish students made it their mission to meet and talk to Jewish students their age in order to bridge the gaps dividing them, especially after the history of extreme experience. As we got to know the Polish students, they seemed very similar to us. They liked the same movies and music, their families and their values and their goals are the same as ours and although they told us that many of their grandparents, who had lived in Poland during the Holocaust, were alive and still had a strong dislike of Jews. These students tried to encourage their grandparents to think differently and made it their goal to do so. It was so interesting when we went to see the movie *The Pianist* in Poland with Polish students and heard their reaction.

Edmund Masojada, the son of Felicia Masojada, also joined us on the trip and made a significant impression on the students with his speech about how his mother and Ludwik Wrodarczyk saved me and my brother when the police were searching for Jews who had escaped the slaughter in the market square in Rokitno.

In Poland we visited concentration camps, including Auschwitz, Birkenau, Treblinka and Majdanek, and historic Jewish places such as the site of the Warsaw ghetto and old cemeteries. We lit candles, we cried and we prayed. It was a powerful and emotional experience for the teenagers from the United States and Canada. They will be able to educate their peers about the Holocaust and fight those who would deny its history, while at the same time forging a dynamic link with Israel. For them it was a journey from darkness to light. For me, marching toward Birkenau carrying the flag of Israel was very significant, first of all for encouraging the young generation to remember the departed and give them the dignity they deserved, and for proclaiming that the Holocaust was not the end of the Jewish people.

These students have joined a chorus of people who have asked me to publish my memoirs. One such student was Craig Dershowitz, a writer who helped edit my book. He told me, "It is imperative that your story be written with as much care, accuracy, respect and power as possible. I hope that by putting your story into a book you might relieve some of your burden and some of your pain."

I pledge to continue my activity in telling my story for my perished mother, father and young brother. They can't speak, so I must.

The Search for My Family Tree

Not long ago I decided that in addition to writing my memoirs, I would undertake research into my family genealogy. This research has been difficult, but the importance of my dual task – to establish my Jewish ancestry and to leave a record for my grandchildren – kept me going. I started with the very little that I remember about my family background and moved from there into the unknown, one step at a time. I worked from the present back to the past, gathering facts from the elderly generation who survived the Holocaust. I checked for information in the Polish archives and collected pictures. I interviewed my relatives in Israel, Brazil, Canada and Russia. I dreamt of flying off to the far-away places that had been under the yellow stars, to my town of Rokitno, where I spent my childhood, to walk in the footsteps of my ancestors, and finally, my brother Samuel and I went for a five-day visit to our shtetl. We wanted to ensure that our search for our family roots was complete. We will preserve our history for future generations.

The *Levin* (Lewin) family comes from Rokitno, Volyn. The town's population – approximately 5,000 when I was born in 1932 – was about one-third Jewish. Many of the Jews traded in grain, wood, hides; some exported dry mushrooms and hops for making beer. The others worked in various trades, earning their livelihood from people in the surrounding villages and towns – among them Sarny, Rovno, Kovel, Lutsk and Lokachy. The Jewish community of Rokitno was Orthodox and observant, with two synagogues.

Rokitno was close to the 1939 border with the USSR; it was the last stop of the railway line on the Polish side. My great-grandfather on my father's side, reb Shraga Faivish Levin, was a rabbi and shochet (ritual slaughterer), first in the old village of Rokitno and then in the new town of Rokitno that was founded in 1901. In 1913, my grandfather, Sheptl Levin, was chosen to go to Eretz Israel to buy land on behalf of Jews in Rokitno who planned to move there.

The *Berengoltz* family (my mother's family) came from the village of Kupichev, in the region of Kovel, Volyn. The village contained both Jewish and Czech communities and I remember that there was a Christian Orthodox church. I visited Kupichev with my Aunt Roza much later when she visited me in Vladimir-Volynsky. By then the Jews had all been killed in the Holocaust and the Czechs had all returned to Czechoslovakia.

The *Zeitlin* family (my wife's family) came from the small town of Senno, in the Vitebsk (Vitsyebsk) region of Belarus. The first recorded settlement of Jews in Belarus dates back to the fourteenth century, when Belarus was region of Poland-Lithuania. At the beginning of Soviet rule in Belorussia in 1919, Jews lived in relative harmony with their Belorusian, Russian, Polish and Ukrainian neighbours. The Jews of Belarus maintained Yiddish as their main language.

The *Halpern* family (my son-in-law's family) comes from Bialystok in Belarus, a prominent Jewish community that dates back to the 1800s. The percentage of the population in the city at that time ranged between 50 and 75 per cent – Bialystok had the highest percentage of Jews in the populations among all the major cities in Poland and the highest number of synagogues per capita in the country.

Glossary

Armia Krajowa (Polish) Also known as AK or the Home Army. Formed in February 1942, the Armia Krajowa was the largest Polish resistance movement in German-occupied Poland in World War II. Although the organization has been criticized for antisemitism and some factions were even guilty of killing Jews, it is also true that the AK established a Section for Jewish Affairs in February 1942 that collected information about what was happening to Jews in Poland, centralized contacts between Polish and Jewish military organizations and supported the Relief Council for Jews in Poland. Members of the AK also supported the Jewish revolt during the Warsaw Ghetto Uprising in 1943, both outside the ghetto walls and by joining Jewish fighters inside the ghetto. Between 1942 and 1945, hundreds of Jews joined the AK.

Betar Zionist youth movement founded by Revisionist Zionist leader Ze'ev Jabotinsky in 1923 to promote the development of a new generation of Zionist activists based on the ideals of courage, self-respect, military training, defence of Jewish life and property, and settlement in Israel leading to the establishment of a Jewish state in British Mandate Palestine. In 1934, Betar membership in Poland numbered over 40,000. The Betar branch that Alex Levin and his three older brother belonged to was founded in Rokitno in 1928. During the 1930s and 1940s, as antisemitism increased and the Nazis launched their murderous campaign against the Jews of Europe, Betar rescued thousands of Jews by organizing illegal immigration to British Mandate Palestine. The Betar Movement today, closely aligned with Israel's right-wing Likud party, remains involved in supporting Jewish and Zionist activism around the world.

blitzkrieg (German; literally: lightning war) The term used to describe the attack of an all-mechanized force (infantry, armour and air) that concentrates on a small section of the enemy front and then moves forward without ensuring the security of its flank. The term can also refer to the period of Germany's "lightning attack" on Western Europe in the early part of World War II.

cheder (Hebrew; literally: room) An Orthodox Jewish elementary school that teaches the fundamentals of Jewish religious observance and textual study as well as the Hebrew language.

Chmielnicki Massacre In 1648, the Cossacks – members of various ethnic groups in southern Russia, Ukraine and Siberia – launched a series of military campaigns to free the Ukraine from Polish domination and establish their own rule in the region. Led by Bohdan Chmielmicki, the Cossacks instigated a brutal uprising against the Jews by telling people that the Poles had sold them to the Jews as slaves. The Cossacks responded by slaughtering tens of thousands of Jews during 1648–49 in what came to be known as the Chmielnicki Massacre. Historians estimate the death toll at about 100,000, with the additional destruction of almost three hundred Jewish communities.

cholent (Yiddish) A traditional Jewish slow-cooked pot stew usually eaten as the main course at the festive Shabbat lunch on Saturdays after the synagogue service and on other Jewish holidays. For Jews of eastern-European descent, the basic ingredients of *cholent* are meat, potatoes, beans and barley.

commissar A Communist Party official assigned to Soviet army units to transmit Party principles and ensure Party loyalty. At different times in the USSR's history, the role of the commissar was very powerful – they operated outside the military hierarchy and reported directly to Party leaders. During the German invasion of the Soviet Union in World War II, commissars were vital in boosting morale among the troops by reinforcing Communist party ideology and preventing dissension in the ranks.

Cuban Missile Crisis The October 1962 Cold War confrontation between the Soviet Union and the United States over missiles that the USSR had based in Cuba. Amid US fears of a Communist foothold in Fidel Castro's Cuba, Cuban fears of a second US invasion following the failed Bay of Pigs incursion in April 1961, and Soviet concerns over losing their one Communist presence in Latin America, Soviet premier Nikita Khrushchev launched a plan in the summer of 1962 to install strategic ballistic missiles in Cuba. In retaliation, US president John F. Kennedy imposed a naval blockade on Cuba in October and declared that any missile launched from Cuba would warrant a full-scale US nuclear attack on the Soviet Union. After two weeks of extreme tension and fears of nuclear war on both sides, an agreement was reached: the missile sites in Cuba would be dismantled in exchange for a US commitment not to invade Cuba. The Soviet ships carrying missiles to Cuba turned back and the crisis ended.

Doctors' Plot An alleged conspiracy by a group of doctors – most of them Jewish – to eliminate the top leadership of the Soviet Union by poisoning them. The accusations in 1953 against the "assassins in white coats" were an escalation of Stalin's campaign against Soviet Jews that began in 1948 and were accompanied by press coverage that produced antisemitic hysteria throughout the country. Stalin planned to use the Doctors' Plot to instigate a major purge directed against Jews and others in the Soviet Union. Fortunately for the accused, Stalin died only days before their trial was about to begin. A month after his death in March 1953, the newspaper *Pravda* declared that the case had been fabricated and that the doctors had been released.

First Ukrainian Front The victorious and much-decorated Red Army formation made up of ten different armies that from 1943 to 1945 fought and overcame German forces, pushing them back through the Ukrainian areas of the USSR and then westward into Poland and Germany itself. Initially called the Voronezh Front, the front was renamed in October 1943 to reflect the westward advance of the Red Army. The 13th Army of the First Ukrainian Front passed through and liberated the area near Rokitno where Alex Levin was hiding in January 1944.

ghetto A confined residential area for Jews. The term originated in Venice, Italy in 1516, with a law requiring all Jews to live on a segregated, gated island known as Ghetto Nuovo. Throughout the Middle Ages in Europe, Jews were often forcibly confined to gated Jewish neighborhoods. During the Holocaust, the Nazis forced Jews to live in crowded and unsanitary conditions in a dilapidated district of a city. Most ghettoes in Poland were enclosed by brick walls or wooden fences with barbed wire.

Haggadah (Hebrew; literally: telling) A book of readings that lays out the order of the Passover seder service and recounts the biblical exodus from slavery.

halutzim (Hebrew) Pioneers. Agricultural immigrants who moved to pre-state Israel to help clear the land, plant trees and drain marshes to establish settlements and build self-sustaining communities; *halutzim* are primarily associated with the wave of immigration known as the Third Aliyah (1919–1923) that followed in the wake of World War I and the establishment of the British Mandate in Palestine.

Jewish Anti-Fascist Committee (JAFC) A group established by Soviet authorities in April 1942 to drum up political and material support for the Soviet struggle against Nazi Germany from Jewish communities in the West. Solomon Mikhoels, popular actor and director of the Moscow Jewish State Theatre, was chairman and the committee had its own Yiddish-language newspaper, *Eynikayt* (Unity). In 1943 Solomon Mikhoels and writer Itzik Feffer raised millions of dollars for the USSR's war effort on a seven-month official tour of North America and Great Britain. After the war, the JAFC became a focal point for Soviet Jews and planned to publish a so-called Black Book that documented the Nazis' anti-Jewish crimes. This contradicted official Soviet policy that Nazi atrocities were committed against all Soviet citizens, with no specific reference to Jews. As the situation for Soviet Jews sharply deteriorated in 1948 and an ideological campaign of persecution ramped up, JAFC members became targets of the Soviet regime. Mikhoels was murdered in November 1948 and other members were arrested, tried and executed in purges over the next four years.

Jewish Autonomous Region Region established by the Soviet authorities in 1934 in the remote Soviet Far East bordering China. The idea behind the Jewish Autonomous Region was to create a new "Soviet Zion," where a proletarian Jewish culture could be developed within a socialist context. Yiddish, rather than Hebrew, would be the national language; and a new socialist literature and arts would replace religion as the primary expression of culture. At the time it was created, Jewish Communists concurred with Stalin's vision for incorporating or "co-opting" ethnic identities as part of a greater Soviet socialist vision and argued that a Soviet Jewish homeland would act as an ideological alternative to Zionism. Early efforts were made to encourage Jews to move into the area, with some 17,000 Jews moving there throughout the 1930s – Alex Levin's Aunt Roza among them. The experiment ground to a halt during Stalin's purges, however, when Jewish leaders were arrested and executed, and Yiddish schools were shut down. World War II brought an abrupt end to official support for Jewish immigration to the region.

Judenrat (German, plural Judenräte) Jewish Council. A group of Jewish leaders appointed by the Germans to administer and provide services to the local Jewish population under occupation and carry out German orders. The Judenräte appeared to be self-governing entities, but were under complete German control. The Judenräte faced difficult and complex moral decisions under brutal conditions and remain a contentious subject. The chairmen had to decide whether to comply or refuse to comply with German demands. Some were killed by the Nazis for refusing, while others committed suicide. Jewish officials who advocated compliance thought that cooperation might save at least some Jews. Some who denounced resistance efforts did so because they believed that armed resistance would bring death to the entire community.

KGB The Russian abbreviation of Komitet Gosudarstvennoy Bezopasnosti (Committee for State Security), the KGB functioned as the Soviet Union's security agency, secret police and intelligence agency from 1954 to 1991. The organization operated with a military hierarchy in its stated dual purpose of simultaneously defending the USSR from external dangers from foreign powers and the Communist Party from perceived dangers within. Under Stalin, the pursuit of imagined conspiracies against the state became a central focus and the KGB played a critical role in suppressing political dissent. In 1967, the year that Alex Levin was forced to resign from the Soviet army, Yuri Andropov became the longest serving and most influential KGB chairman – under his leadership, the organization increased its focus on combating any and every perceived "ideological subversion," no matter how minor.

Kaddish (Aramaic; literally: holy) Also known as the Mourners' Prayer, Kaddish is said as part of mourning rituals in Jewish prayer services as well as at funerals and memorials.

Khrushchev, Nikita First Secretary of the Communist Party of the Soviet Union from 1953 to 1964, Nikita Khrushchev stunned Party members when he denounced the excesses of the Stalin era and Stalin's cult of personality in 1956. Khrushchev's regime was characterized not only by de-Stalinization of the USSR but by a foreign policy that espoused peaceful co-existence with the West. By the early 1960s, bitter power struggles within the leadership of the Communist Party, a political split with Communist leadership in China, and Soviet humiliation over the 1962 Cuban Missile Crisis led to Khruschev's ouster in October 1964.

kosher (Hebrew) Fit to eat according to Jewish dietary laws. Observant Jews follow a system of rules known as Kashruth that regulates what can be eaten, how food is prepared and how meat and poultry are slaughtered. Food is kosher when it is deemed fit for consumption according to this system of rules. *See also* shochet.

mezuzah (Hebrew; literally: doorpost) The small piece of parchment inscribed with specific Hebrew texts from the Torah, usually enclosed in a decorative casing, that is placed on the doorframes of homes of observant Jews.

Organisation Todt A construction and civil engineering group named for its founder, Fritz Todt, that undertook major civilian and military projects under the Nazis. It began as a quasi-governmental agency but in 1942 it was absorbed by the German government, becoming part of the Ministry of Armaments and War Production under Albert Speer. It made extensive use of forced and slave labour. In Rokitno this labour entailed repairing the roads and railways damaged in the blitzkrieg, log-cutting and working in the glass factory or the fields.

OVIR The Office of Visas and Registration of the Soviet Ministry of the Interior – the office to which Soviet citizens wishing to emigrate had to apply. During the Soviet era, an application to the OVIR for permission to leave the USSR had to be accompanied by numerous documents (including character references from one's place of employment; approval from the local Communist Party offices and from one's professional union; permission from one's parents, regardless of age; permission from a former spouse in the case of divorce). At the same time, the act of applying for an exit visa often created economic and social problems for the applicants (for example, they often had to quit their jobs). OVIR held a great deal of power over Soviet Jews wishing to emigrate from the USSR – some were allowed to leave but many were refused permission to emigrate instantly, and still others would have their files blocked for years in OVIR without explanation.

partisans Members of irregular military forces or resistance movements formed to oppose armies of occupation. During World War II there were a number of different partisan groups that opposed both the Nazis and their collaborators in several countries. In the area where Alex Levin was hiding, there were Belarusian, Ukrainian and Jewish partisans, as well as Soviet partisans directed by the Soviet government and the Red Army. In reality, the term partisan could include highly organized, almost paramilitary groups like the Red Army partisans, ad hoc groups bent more on survival than resistance and roving groups of bandits who plundered what they could from all sides.

Passover (in Hebrew, Pesach) A major festival of the Jewish calendar which takes place over eight days in the spring. One of the main observance of the holiday is to recount the story of Exodus, of the Jews flight from slavery in Egypt, at a ritual meal called a seder. The name itself refers to the fact that God "passed over" the houses of the Jews when he set about slaying the firstborn sons of Egypt as the last of the ten plagues aimed at convincing Pharaoh to free the Jews.

Piłsudski, Marshal Józef De facto dictator of the Second Polish Republic from 1926 to 1935, Józef Piłsudski is considered to be a hero who was largely responsible for achieving Poland's independence in 1918 after more than a century of being partitioned by various major powers. Piłsudski's regime was notable for the improvement in the situation of ethnic minorities, including Poland's large Jewish population. He followed a policy of "state-assimilation" whereby citizens were judged not by their ethnicity but by their loyalty to the state. Many Polish Jews felt that their situation improved under Piłsudski and felt that he was key to keeping the antisemitic currents in Poland in check; many voted for him and actively participated in his political bloc. With his death in 1935 the quality of life of Poland's Jews deteriorated once again. Until his death, he also managed to keep both Hitler and Stalin at bay, resisting Germany's attempts to pressure Poland into an alliance against the USSR and extending a Soviet-Polish nonaggression treaty until 1945.

Polesie (Polish) Also known as Polesia. Polesie is the largest swampy lowland area in Europe that lies mainly within present-day Belarus and Ukraine but also reaches into parts of Poland and Russia. It is a vast expanse of saturated sandy lowlands, low-lying bogs and marshes, and dense pine forests intersected by a network of rivers. About one-third of the region is forested with a mixture of pine, white spruce, birch, alder, oak and aspen. This is the simultaneously rich and treacherous terrain that Alex and Samuel Levin survived in for almost eighteen months.

ruble The unit of currency in the Soviet Union, the ruble was also the unit of currency in the Russian Empire and remains so today in the Russian Federation.

shochet (Hebrew; also, Yiddish, shoyket) Ritual slaughterer. A man conversant with the religious teaching of Kashruth, trained to slaughter animals painlessly and check the meat afterward to be sure it is kosher. *See also* kosher.

seder (Hebrew; literally: order) A ritual family meal celebrated on the first two nights of the eight day festival of Passover in the Diaspora, and on the first night only in modern Israel.

Shabbat (Hebrew; in Yiddish, *Shabbes, Shabbos*) Sabbath. The weekly day of rest beginning Friday at sundown and ending Saturday at sundown ushered in by the lighting of candles on Friday night and the recitation of blessings over wine and challah (egg bread); a day of celebration as well as prayer, it is customary to eat three festive meals, attend synagogue services and refrain from doing any work or travelling.

shtetl (Yiddish) Small town. A small village or town with a predominantly Jewish population that existed before World War II in Central and Eastern Europe.

Six-Day War The armed conflict between Israel and the neighbouring states of Egypt, Jordan, and Syria that took place from June 5–10, 1967. In response to the creation of an alliance between Egypt, Syria and Jordan and the mobilization of troops by Egypt's leader Gamal Nasser along Israel's borders, Israel launched a preemptive attack. In the days that followed, Israeli forces drove the armies back and occupied the Sinai Peninsula, Gaza Strip, West Bank and Golan Heights. Israel also reunited Jerusalem, the eastern half of which Jordan had controlled since the 1948–1949 war. The Six-Day War was viewed as an enormous military victory for Israel, but did not lead to similar diplomatic successes or peace in the region.

son of the regiment The term used for orphaned boys who were adopted by Soviet army regiments and served in uniform.

Sovietization The USSR's policies of imposing ideologically motivated changes to political, economic, social and cultural life in
occupied territories. These changes included confiscation, nationalization and redistribution of private and state-owned Polish
property, and discrimination against and outright persecution of
capitalists and others considered dangerous to the Soviet regime.

SS The abbreviation for Schutzstaffel (Defense Corps), the SS began as
Adolf Hitler's elite corps of personal bodyguards, but under Hein-
rich Himmler the SS expanded to gain control of all of Germany's
police forces. The organization divided into the Allgemeine-SS
(General SS) and the Waffen-SS (Armed SS). The main compo-
nent of the General SS, which primarily dealt with policing and
the enforcement of Nazi racial policies in Germany and the Nazi-
occupied countries, was the Reichssicherheitshauptamt (RSHA,
the Central Office of Reich Security), the umbrella organization
that included the Gestapo (Geheime Staatspolizei). The SS ran the
concentration and death camps, with all their associated economic enterprises, and also fielded its own Waffen SS military divi-
sions, including some recruited from the occupied countries.

Stalin's Antisemitic Campaign Between 1948 and 1953 Stalin embarked on a campaign against elements within the USSR that he
believed posed a threat to the homogeneity of Soviet society. The
main targets of this campaign were prominent Jewish community
members, writers and artists. As Stalin's paranoia increased, the
campaign culminated in two events in 1952–1953: the so-called
Night of the Murdered Poets, which refers to the night of August
12–13, 1952, when thirteen prominent Yiddish writers were executed, and the early 1952 "Doctors' Plot." Stalin's death in March
1953 brought an end to his virulent antisemitic campaign. *See also*
Doctors' Plot.

Suvorov Military Schools Military boarding schools named for eigh-
teenth-century military leader General Alexander Vasilyevich

Suvorov that provide teenage boys with an education focused on military subjects and training. The Suvorov Military Academies started off as state shelters for the large number of children who had been orphaned in World War II. The schools were created in 1943 in the tradition of the famous cadet corps first established in Saint Petersburg in 1731.

Tarbut (Hebrew; literally: culture) A Zionist network of secular Hebrew-language schools – kindergartens, elementary schools, secondary schools and adult education programs – that operated primarily in Poland, Romania and Lithuania between World War I and World War II. The name Tarbut references the schools, secular, cultural approach to Jewish studies as opposed to religious instruction. The educational institutions under the Tarbut umbrella also included teachers' seminaries, lending libraries and a publishing house that produced pedagogical materials, textbooks and children's periodicals. The Tarbut school in Rokitno was founded in the 1920s.

TASS (Telegrafnoye agentstvo Sovetskogo Soyuza, or Telegraph Agency of the Soviet Union) The central agency for collection and distribution of internal and international news for all Soviet newspapers and radio and television stations. It had a monopoly on official state information.

Treaty of Non-Aggression between Germany and the USSR Colloquially known as the Molotov-Ribbentrop Pact for Soviet foreign minister Vyacheslav Molotov and German foreign minister Joachim von Ribbentrop, this treaty was signed on August 24, 1939. The main provisions of the pact stipulated that the two countries would not go to war with each other and that they would both remain neutral if either one was attacked by a third party. One of the key components of the treaty was the division of various independent countries – including Poland – into Nazi and Soviet spheres of influence. The Nazis breached the pact by launching a major offensive against the Soviet Union on June 22, 1941. These events that led to the occupations of Rokitno, first by the Soviets and then by the Germans.

Ukrainische Hilfspolizei (German) Ukrainian Auxiliary Police. The Ukrainian auxiliary police force that collaborated with the Nazis in the implementation of the "Final Solution" against the Jews and in controlling non-Jewish opposition to the Germans.

Zhdanovschina Named after the USSR's Communist Party Central Committee Secretary Andrei Zhdanov, one of the most powerful Soviet officials during the Stalinist era, the Zhdanovschina was the campaign of internal post-war cultural and social repression in the USSR. Artists, writers, musicians and any other individuals with a role in shaping opinion had to conform to strict new Party guidelines and many were persecuted, arrested and executed as "cosmopolitans" and "bourgeois individualists." The campaign specifically targeted Jews – so-called rootless cosmopolitans. Zhdanov's policies were also influential in the realm of foreign policy, encapsulating a hardening anti-Western policy following World War II that saw the world as being in two camps – communist and imperialist – with no possibility of co-existence.

Maps & Photographs

Arctic Circle

Kandalashka

NORWAY

FINLAND

SWEDEN

Leningrad

USSR

ESTONIA

LATVIA

DENMARK

MOSCOW

LITHUANIA

EAST PRUSSIA
(GERMANY)

BERLIN

POLAND

Voronezh

GERMANY

WARSAW

Sarny

Vladimir-Volynsky

Rokitno

Kiev

Vistula

Sandomierz

Dubno

Lubny

CZECHOSLVAKIA

Brody

VIENNA

AUSTRIA

HUNGARY

ITALY

ROMANIA

Odessa

YUGOSLAVIA

Evpatoria

ROME

BULGARIA

1937 Borders

0   400   800 km

0   400 miles

© 2009 The Azrieli Foundation

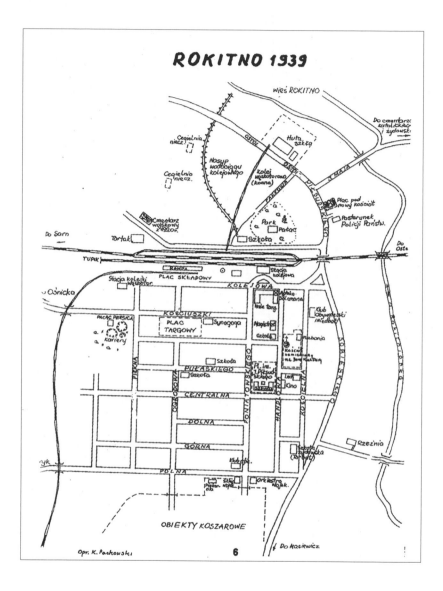

ROKITNO 1939

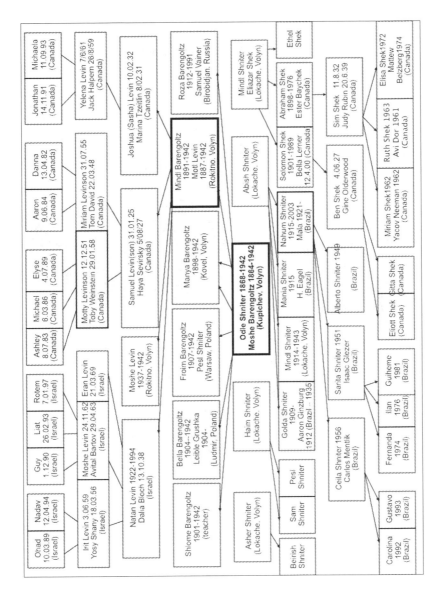

Alex Levin's Family Tree

Alex Levin's parents, Mindl Barengoltz and Mordechai Levin.

Alex's mother's family. Standing left to right: Her sister Roza, her brother Shlomo, her sister Bella, her brother Froim, her sister Mania, Mindl holding Alex's eldest brother, Natan (age three); seated: Grandmother Hava holding Alex's brother Samuel (age one) and Grandfather Moshe holding Mania's son, Yone.

Alex's youngest brother, Moishe, who was killed by the Nazis at the age of five in the Rokitno Massacre, August 26, 1942. The text on the back of the picture reads: "20/VI/1938, Moshe, 11 months old. We send the 'small gardener.' He likes flowers very much. He is sending Aunt Roza a bouquet."

Piłsudski Street, where Alex Levin lived in Rokitno before the war.

Marketplace in Rokitno, the site of the Rokitno Massacre.

Alex with his Red Army liberator, Rokitno, January 1944.

Alex as a "son of the regiment" in the Red Army, Sarny, February 1944.

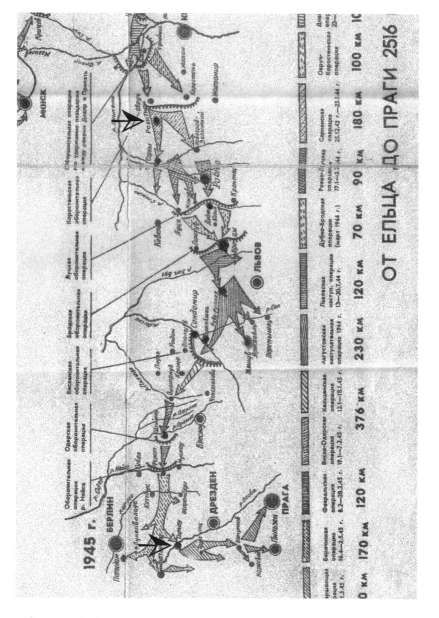

Militant Road of the 13th Soviet army in World War II, 1941–1945. Alex joined the
unit as a messenger boy for Field Hospital No. 2408 in Rokitno and stayed with
them to Torgau, Germany.

YAD VASHEM – JEROZOLIMA
„Sprawiedliwi wśród Narodów Świata"

Felicja Masojada c. Michała
Nr t. 8930

ks. Ludwik Wrodarczyk s. Karola
Nr t. 8930A

Tytuły zostały nadane pośmiertnie 3.08.2000

1

2   3

1 Felicja Masojada and Father Ludwik Wrodarczyk, "Righteous Gentiles" who helped Alex and Samuel while they were in hiding near the village of Okopy.

2 Solomon Mikhoels, chairman of the Jewish Anti-Fascist Committee in the Soviet Union.

3 A monument at the gravesite of Solomon Mikhoels put up in commemoration of the fiftieth anniversary of his murder by Stalin's secret police in 1948. Donskoi cemetery, Moscow, 1998.

1 Alex a new cadet in the Suvorov Military School, Voronezh, 1946.

2 Alex (right) on vacation with his best friend at cadet school, Novik Sidorov, and Novik's mother, Tamara Akimovna Sidorova. Moscow, 1946.

3 Alex's class at the cadet school, 1950. Alex is in the middle, between the two officers.

Alex's graduation photo, Suvorov Military School, Voronezh, 1951.

First reunion of Alex's class from the Suvorov Military School, Voronezh, 1953.

Lieutenant Alex Levin in the 51st Motorized Infantry Regiment in the town of Kandalaksha, above the Arctic Circle, in 1954.

1 Captain Alex Levin at the Military Academy of the Civilian Home Front and Transportation, Leningrad, 1960.

2 Alex's reunion with his brother Samuel (right) after thirty years, Moscow, 1974.

3 Alex with his wife, Marina, and Marina's family. Standing left to right: Marina's sister, Vera, Alex and Marina. Seated in front are Marina's father, Aaron Grigorievich Zeitlin, and her mother, Rita Moiseevna.

Reunion of the three surviving brothers. From left to right: Alex (Joshua), Samuel and Natan. Toronto, 1988.

Alex and Samuel's return to Rokitno in June 1995.

Alex at the monument commemorating the murdered Jews of Rokitno.
Rokitno cemetery, June 1995.

Commemorative monument in Sarny, where 18,000 Jews from Rokitno and surrounding area were murdered in late August 1942.

Reunion of Rokitno Holocaust survivors in Toronto, 1999. From left: Yona Wasserman, Samuel Levin, Alex (Joshua) Levin, Lowa Gamulka and Monek Griever.

Alex (centre) with the March of the Living, Auschwitz-Birkenau, Poland, 2002.

Bat mitzvah of Alex's granddaughter, Michaela Halpern, Toronto, November 12, 2005. Standing from left: Jack Halpern, Alex's son-in-law, Michaela, and Alex's grandson Jonathan. Seated in front: Marina Levin (left) and Alex and Marina's daughter, Yelena Halpern.

Index

The Azrieli Foundation

The Azrieli Foundation was established in 1989 to realize and extend the philanthropic vision of David J. Azrieli, C.M., C.Q., MArch. The Foundation's mission is to support a wide spectrum of initiatives in education and research. The Azrieli Foundation is an active supporter of programs in the fields of Jewish education, the education of architects, scientific and medical research, and education in the arts. The Azrieli Foundation's many well-known initiatives include: the Holocaust Survivor Memoirs Program, which collects, preserves, publishes and distributes the written memoirs of survivors in Canada; the Azrieli Institute for Educational Empowerment, an innovative program successfully working to keep at-risk youth in school; and the Azrieli Fellows Program, which promotes academic excellence and leadership on the graduate level at Israeli universities. Programs sponsored and supported are located in Canada, Israel and the United States.

Israel and Golda Koschitzky Centre for Jewish Studies

In 1989, York University established Canada's first interdisciplinary research centre in Jewish studies. Over the years, the Israel and Golda Koschitzky Centre for Jewish Studies has earned national and international acclaim for its dynamic approach to teaching and research. While embracing Jewish culture and classical study in all its richness, the Centre also has a distinctly modern core, and a strong interest in the study of the Canadian Jewish experience. York was the Canadian pioneer in the study of the Holocaust. The Centre maintains its strong commitment to the study of the Holocaust through the research, teaching, and community involvement of its faculty, its graduate diploma program in Advanced Hebrew and Jewish Studies, and its unique program of Holocaust and anti-racist education – developed in cooperation with the Centre for German and European Studies – for Canadian, German and Polish education students.